Neuro Habits:

Rewire Your Brain to Stop Self-Defeating Behaviors and Make the Right Choice Every Time

By Peter Hollins,
Author and Researcher at
peutehollins.com

D1523434

Table of Contents

Chapter 1. A Peek into the Science of Habits

What is a habit?

You might have worked your way through dozens of old habits today already, before reading this book. You didn't have to really think about any of these activities—the specific way you went about brushing your teeth, making coffee, checking your emails. Sure, the *first* time you ever performed one of these habits you probably had to pay full and focused attention, but after hundreds or even thousands of times repeating the same routines, you now complete them on autopilot. They are, in other words, habitual.

Many of us think of habits in terms of behavior. We try to eliminate bad habits or encourage better ones by using sheer force of willpower. We tend to think of habits as not sticking simply because we're lazy, or we're just not trying hard enough. But the fact is that habits are the external, behavioral manifestations of *internal* brain processes—which have very little to do with willpower.

Habits are there for a reason. They are your brain's shortcuts through life, or what are called "heuristics," mental models used to process the familiar and expected patterns of experience. Habits help us save time and energy. If we can do something automatically and without thinking too hard about it, we save our attention for the truly difficult things. But habits are not just behaviors—they are an external expression of a physical process unfolding in your brain.

The old saying goes, "Neurons that fire together, wire together." This essentially means that when your brain repeats the same patterns over and over again, the neurons responsible are physically and literally "wired" in a fixed way—your habit is physiologically programmed into your brain. Psychologists and neurologists have long understood that there exists a certain neural correlate to our everyday behavior, and that our fixed and routine habits actually map onto similarly fixed physiological structures in the brain.

Understanding exactly how and why habits form in the brain puts us in the best possible position to make real changes. Once we can see how the brain's physiology and biochemistry connects seamlessly to our behavior, we can look with fresh eyes at our actions and the accompanying psychology. We can more effectively change ourselves, whether we want to quit smoking or wake up earlier or get out of the habit of negative self-talk.

Your brain's superpower of neuroplasticity

Your brain possesses a truly marvelous characteristic called neuroplasticity. You were not born with a fully functional brain, but rather with the hardware and *ability to learn*, which then allowed your brain to form connections, to grow, and to acquire knowledge. The neuroplastic brain is one that can change. It's the reason you were able to develop bad habits in the first place; but it's also the reason you'll be able to break them and form new, more beneficial habits.

People are capable of behavioral change. And the brain is capable of *physiological* change to support it. Let's take a closer look:

We'll consider habits in terms of the famous three-part habit loop outlined in Charles Duhigg's book, *The Power of Habit*. You might recognize this model in different forms, and under different names, but its main features are the same.

Part one is the **trigger**. This is a cue or signal that alerts your brain to enter into a kind of autopilot so that a previously learnt behavior can be executed. You know the state of mind you're in when you find yourself pulling the car up to your home with no recollection of the drive you made to get there? This is the state of mind Duhigg is talking about, and a trigger tells your brain to switch into this mode.

A trigger can be a person, a change in the environment, a certain time of day, even a word or symbol. The trigger for one behavior can be the actions of a previous behavior. For example, you always reach for a glass of wine when you get home from work. The trigger is the act of getting home, which basically tells your brain "run the get-a-glass-of-wine program now."

Once you're in this mode, you play out the behavior itself, or the **routine**. Habits are procedural—they're typically a set of behaviors followed step by step, like the four or five little things you always do in the same order when you step into the shower every morning. A trigger can instigate the first behavior in a long string of habits.

The third step is the **reward**, which is what it sounds like: a pleasant outcome that helps to reinforce the behavior so that our brain knows what to return to the next time it encounters the same trigger. Granted, you might not be able to think of much reward in any of the little habits you perform every day, but somewhere along the line, your brain made the judgment that there was something valuable in these behaviors.

Rewards can be small—the feeling that things are right in the world, a sense of order or stability, a feeling of completeness and familiarity. Rewards can even include the removal of something unpleasant or the threat of it.

This loop explains how certain behaviors and habits can carry on even when we rationally and consciously know that they're bad for us, or when we no longer get any immediate satisfaction out of them. For example, it will suddenly be lunchtime, which is the trigger that reminds you to head outside for a smoke break, and before you know it in you're in that half-unconscious autopilot mode. It doesn't matter if you don't really enjoy smoking anymore; at some point, you did, and the sense of reward strengthened the habit.

So, this is what habit formation looks like from the outside, but what's going on in the brain?

Cognitive psychologists and neuroscientists attribute the creation and maintenance of habits to a part of the brain called the basal ganglia. Importantly, this is also a part of the brain associated with emotions, pattern recognition and memory. These brain mechanisms are essential—they give human beings enormous flexibility and freedom to "bank" already mastered routines so that they can be done on autopilot while the rest of the brain focuses intently on more important issues.

This remainder of the brain is broadly the prefrontal cortex, which is associated with a host of higher order and executive functions like making conscious decisions, planning, solving problems or being creative. While you may use this part of your brain when learning something new, once you've mastered it, the routine is delegated to the basal ganglia. This kind of "thinking" is almost not thinking at all—the brain is more or less asleep or offline, running an old routine that takes barely any mental effort or brainpower.

Isn't it remarkable, that your brain has figured out a way to perform all these complex activities without even being aware of it, and without spending any extra cognitive energy? Sadly, the same mechanism that entrenches useful habits does the same with unhelpful ones. In fact, neuroscientists at MIT have identified the part of the brain that acts as a "switch" between the two modes.

In experiments with rats, the scientists were able to essentially turn a habit on or off by manipulating a part of the prefrontal cortex, called the infralimbic (IL) cortex. This can be thought of as a tiny part of the higher brain that is still engaged, even though the rest of the basal ganglia is following through with a largely automatic habit. The researchers were interested in how this knowledge could be used to treat people with mental conditions like obsessive-compulsive disorder, but the potential for helping people break bad habits in a broader sense is also promising.

The scientists concluded that the IL was responsible for determining which ingrained habitual behavior patterns would be expressed in any moment. Old habits may not be performed, for example, but they are still there, and can be picked up again if necessary, like riding a bike. Various habits are all stored completely intact, but the IL helps to retrieve whichever ones are necessary – helped by certain cues and triggers.

Unfortunately, it's not clear how humans could directly stimulate their own IL cortices to replicate these studies. But the results do seem to suggest that there is some scope to "switching off" bad habits and replacing them with better ones—with the assistance of the brain. If we know that the basal ganglia works to convert new routines into automatic habits, and that the IL cortex can act as a sort of online monitoring system to control that process, then we can take steps to learn new and better habits and drop bad ones.

Let's return to the three-step model: some studies have shown that the triggers for automatic behaviors are often environmental. For example, we always get out of bed, put on our slippers and reach for our phone in the same way when we're in our own homes, but somehow, being in a hotel room for the night disrupts all these old routines. Suddenly, you are paying conscious attention to what is ordinarily unconscious and automatic; your IL is in charge, and not your basal ganglia.

Knowing this, it makes sense to try to break habits by disrupting their triggers and cues. Many people find they can successfully break bad habits when on vacation for this very reason. It's even better if all the old rewards that keep the behavior in place are also removed with a change in environment.

In the chapters that follow, we'll look at scientific research into the physiological and neurochemical phenomena underpinning the process of forming, maintaining and breaking habits, and converting these into actionable insights that improve our habits. The goal is to find concrete ways to transform our own habits in real life. Though it's not always possible to stick electrodes into our brain to literally change the structures there, we can work from the outside in, altering our behavior to support our inbuilt processes and replace bad habits with better ones.

In this book we'll be taking a proactive perspective, because it's never too late to break a habit, or learn something new. Neuroplasticity is something we can work with throughout our lives, and the key is to get a handle on the structure of habits and how they work in our lives. Once we understand the neuroscience of habits, we can take practical steps to remove cues and triggers, as well as eliminate rewards for undesirable behaviors so that we can gear ourselves up for healthier, more productive habits instead.

One thing we'll set aside for now is the idea that breaking bad habits is about morality, willpower or force. We are all human, and breaking old habits takes effort and conscious intention. It's not easy! But at the same time, it's something that we can and should aspire to.

What happens in the brain when habits form?

We've looked briefly at the two broad parts of the brain responsible for two different states of mind—conscious, aware control mode and habitual "autopilot" mode, situated in the IL in the prefrontal cortex and the basal ganglia, respectively. But of course, the brain is not a static entity; it's dynamic. The cells of the brain are in constant communication with each other via brain chemicals called neurotransmitters.

Neurons produce neurotransmitters, which act as chemical messengers that travel all throughout the brain, and from the brain to the spinal cord, muscles, and every part of the body. The ebb and flow of specialized neurotransmitters has just as important a role in the formation and maintenance of habits as brain structures do—they work together. You may already be aware of neurotransmitters like dopamine and serotonin, and their effect on mood, motivation, and even addictive behavior.

Naturally, these neurotransmitters feature heavily in the way we form habits, good and bad. Let's take a look at an important brain chemical, dopamine. This neurotransmitter is a key chemical messenger in the parts of the brain associated with reward and pleasure. Whenever you feel good, you can be sure dopamine is playing a role somewhere. Whether it's sex, good food, achieving a goal, or even drug use, the body releases dopamine which helps the brain to associate these activities with pleasurable feelings.

This is why dopamine is sometimes said to act as a reward molecule—it drives us to repeat behaviors that have felt good in the past, strengthening associations and habits. If you eat a delicious meal, your neurons will produce a shot of dopamine that will make you feel great. This good feeling is essentially a reward that cements your perception of the behavior, making you want to repeat it in future when you see a cue for that same meal again. Dopamine is a powerful driver of the three-step habit formation loop.

On the other hand, dysregulated dopamine levels can have serious effects on our memory, focus, mood and even movement. When our ordinary reward-reinforcement cycles are broken, we may find ourselves gravitating toward things that may feel pleasurable, but are actually bad for us.

In fact, many psychologists have noted that those who develop addictions often have low dopamine levels to start with, and may be so strongly attracted to drugs, alcohol, food, overspending, gambling or sex to bolster chronically flagging dopamine levels. Dopamine tells the brain what activities were pleasurable, and which to repeat. People with low dopamine levels may pursue behaviors that trigger dopamine release, even though it's ultimately harmful for them—in other words, a healthy reward system may become dysregulated.

Low dopamine is associated not only with addiction, but with a range of mental challenges: anxiety, mood swings, low motivation, low libido, depression, low self-esteem and even suicidal thoughts can all result from dopamine deficiency. Because neurotransmitters affect the entire body, dysregulation can manifest with a range of symptoms.

Neurotransmitters like dopamine affect how we feel, but also how we behave. As certain behaviors are reinforced through reward mechanisms, habits become ingrained with time. Our habits are what we do day in and day out, and our actions shape our world and determine how the world responds in turn to us. It's no exaggeration, then, to say that our brain chemistry affects our habits, and our habits create *who we are as people.*

Dopamine is a major brain chemical, since it drives so much of our habitual and reward-focused behavior, but it's not the only chemical underpinning both our lived experience and our persistent behaviors. Others include serotonin, glutamate, epinephrine, norepinephrine and GABA.

Let's return to the two brain "modes" from the previous section: conscious, focused and goal-directed behavior (connected with the prefrontal cortex and IL) and the autopilot habit mode (connected with the basal ganglia). The first is dynamic, intelligent and flexible, but takes a lot of mental energy, while the second is based on past experiences, so it can run efficiently without spending much mental energy at all.

We've seen that special areas of the prefrontal cortex can act as a "switch" to determine which mode the brain should operate in, but this process is actually managed by important neurochemicals, which are the messengers or chemical go-betweens that make it all happen. Dopamine features here, but so does serotonin, another "feel-good" brain chemical.

Most research into dopamine has tended to show that the neurotransmitter increases habit formation in mice during experiments, whereas destroying areas of the brain that produce dopamine can actually impair the learning or habit-forming process. But it's not such a straightforward relationship—other research has shown that lowering dopamine levels can also be associated with being better able to control habits. Why? Some have suggested that high dopamine levels can actually help the brain switch into conscious, goal-directed mode and out of habit mode, even though it's in the habit mode that certain behaviors are likely to stimulate the release of dopamine.

It may also be that other neurotransmitters like serotonin *moderate* the balance between goal-oriented mode and habitual mode; in humans, low serotonin might make it harder to switch out of habit mode, and into goal-directed mode. The brain's opioid system, which is connected to the reward system, likewise mediates and shapes the brain's overall balance between the different mental states. These neurotransmitters, then, can be thought of as master controllers and managers of the habit-formation process.

Dopamine and the pleasure principle

Dopamine's role in reinforcing pleasure correlates to one of the most well-known theories concerning human behavior.

Rather, perhaps it's more accurate to say that the studies on dopamine align with this more foundational theory.

Out of all the speculations about the sources of habit, none is more famous than the *pleasure principle*. The reason it's so renowned is because it's also the easiest to understand. The pleasure principle was first raised in public consciousness by the father of psychoanalysis, Sigmund Freud, though researchers as far back as Aristotle in ancient Greece noted how easily we could be manipulated and motivated by pleasure and pain.

The pleasure principle asserts that the human mind does everything it can to seek out pleasure and avoid pain. It doesn't get simpler than that. In that simplicity, we find some of life's most universal and predictable motivators.

The pleasure principle is employed by the *id*, which is how Freud identifies one of the psyche's three governing entities (the others being the ego and the superego). For our purposes, we'll focus only on the id. The id houses our desires and physical "needs." It doesn't have any sense of restraint. It is primal and unfiltered. It goes after whatever it can to meet our body's urges for happiness and fulfillment. Anything that causes pleasure is felt by the brain in the same way, whether it's a tasty meal or a drug. An apt illustration of this principle, in fact, is a drug addict who will stop at nothing to get another taste of narcotics.

There are a few rules that govern the pleasure principle and how we are motivated.

Every decision we make is based on gaining pleasure or avoiding pain. This is the common habit for every person on earth. No matter what we do in the course of our day, it all comes down to the pleasure principle. You raid the refrigerator for snacks because you crave the taste and feel of certain food. You get a haircut because you think it will make you more attractive to someone else, which will make you happy, which is pleasure.

Conversely, you wear a protective mask while you're using a blowtorch because you want to avoid sparks flying into your face and eyes, because that will be painful. If we trace all of our decisions back, whether short-term or long-term, we'll find that they all stem from a small set of pleasures or pains.

People work harder to avoid pain than to get pleasure. While everyone wants pleasure as much as they can get it, their habit to avoid pain is actually far stronger. The instinct to survive a threatening situation is more immediate than eating your favorite candy bar, for instance. So when faced with the prospect of pain, the brain will work harder to avoid it than it would to gain access to pleasure.

For example, imagine you're standing in the middle of a desert road. In front of you is a treasure chest filled with money and outlandishly expensive jewelry that could set you up financially for the rest of your life. But there's also an out-of-control semi careening toward it. You're probably going to make the decision to jump away from the truck rather than grab the treasure chest, because your instinct to avoid pain—in this case, certain death—outweighed your desire to gain pleasure.

If you've hit rock bottom and faced a massive amount of pain or discomfort, then you simply must start acting to avoid that in the future. A wounded animal is more motivated than a slightly uncomfortable one.

Our perceptions of pleasure and pain are more powerful drivers than the actual things. When our brain is judging between what will be a pleasant or painful experience, it's working from scenarios that we *think* could result if we took a course of action. In other words, our *perceptions* of pleasure and pain are really what drive the car. And sometimes those perceptions can be flawed. In fact, they are mostly flawed, which explains our tendency to work against our own best interests.

I can think of no better example of this rule than *jalapeño chapulines*. They're a spicy, traditional Mexican snack that's tasty and low in carbs. By the way, *"chapulines"* means "grasshoppers." We're talking chili-flavored grasshoppers. The insects.

Now, you may have no firsthand knowledge of how grasshoppers taste. Maybe you've never tried them. But the *thought* of eating grasshoppers may give you pause. You imagine they'll be repellant to the tongue. You imagine if you take a bite of a grasshopper you'll get grossed out. You might accidentally bite down on an internal grasshopper organ. The *perception* of eating a grasshopper is driving you quickly away from the act of tasting one.

But the fact remains that *you haven't actually tried it yet*. You're working from your *idea* of the repulsion that eating a grasshopper will bring about. Somebody who's actually tried grasshopper-based cuisine may insist to you that they're really *good* when prepared properly. Still, you might not be able to get over your innate perception of what eating an insect would be like.

Pleasure and pain are changed by time. In general, we focus on the here and now: what can I get very soon that will bring me happiness? Also, what is coming up very soon that could be intensely painful that I'll have to avoid? When considering the attainment of comfort, we're more tuned in to what might take place immediately. The pleasure and pain that might happen months or years from now doesn't really register with us—what's most important is whatever's right at our doorstep. Of course, this is another way in which our perceptions are flawed and why we might procrastinate so frequently.

For example, a smoker needs a cigarette. It's the main focus of their current situation. It brings them a certain relief or pleasure. And in about fifteen minutes, they'll be on break so they can enjoy that cigarette. It's the focus of their daily ritual. They're *not* thinking about how smoking a cigarette every time they "need" one could cause painful health problems down the road. That's a distant reality that's not driving their behavior at all. Right now, they need a smoke because they crave one, and they might get a headache immediately if they don't get one.

Emotion beats logic. When it comes to the pleasure principle, your feelings tend to overshadow rational thought. You might know that doing something will be good or bad for you. You'll understand all the reasons why it will be good or bad. You'll get all that. But if your illogical id is so intent on satisfying a certain craving, then it's probably going to win out. And if your id drives you to think that doing something useful will cause too much stress or temporary dissatisfaction, it's going to win there too.

Going back to our smoker, without a doubt they know why cigarettes are bad for one's health. They've read those warnings on the packages. Maybe in school they saw a picture of a corroded lung that resulted from years of smoking. They *know* all the risks they're about to court. But there's that pack right in front of them. And all reason be damned, they're going to have that cigarette. Their emotions oriented toward pleasure win out.

Survival overrides everything. When our survival instinct gets activated, everything else in our psychological and emotional makeup turns off. If a life-threatening situation (or a *perceived* life-threatening situation) arises in our existence, the brain closes down everything else and turns us into a machine whose thoughts and actions are all oriented toward the will to survive.

This shouldn't be surprising when it comes to avoiding painful outcomes. Of *course* you're going to try and jump away from that oncoming semitruck; if you don't, you won't survive. Your system won't let you make that choice—it's going to do everything it can to get you the hell out of the way of that truck.

However, survival can *also* come into play when we're seeking pleasure—even if it means we might slip into harm's way. The most obvious example of this is food. Say you're at a bar and somebody orders a giant plate of nachos loaded with cheese, sour cream, fatty meat, and a bunch of other ingredients that might not be the best dietary choices for you. You *might* be able to resist it. Some people can. But you might not. In fact, you could find yourself eating half the plate before you even know what you've done.

Why? Because you need food to survive. And your brain is telling you there's food in the vicinity, so perhaps you should eat it. Never mind that it's not the best kind of food, nutritionally speaking, that you could opt for at the moment. Your survival instinct is telling you it's time to have those nachos. Your life depends on it.

Our brain chemistry works from these two very basic opposites of pain and pleasure, and some of the circuitry involved has been strengthened or warped by our life experiences.

It's important to understand that research results like these should be interpreted with caution, since they focus mainly on animal behavior in highly artificial laboratory situations. Nevertheless, they do tell us something compelling about the way the brain works when it comes to habits:

that it has a neurochemical basis, and that *it can be changed.*

Understanding the psychology of habits, and learning to form new, positive habits in the place of less healthy ones, starts with the brain and its physiology. Habit formation occurs in three basic steps, which have real, physical effects in the brain in the form of neurotransmitter release.

For example, you might have an unhealthy snacking habit, automatically reaching for something sweet after dinner every night. You know you need to stop guzzling chocolate and candy, and some nights you don't even enjoy these binges, but you can't stop. Willpower doesn't seem to be enough.

There's no need to give up or feel bad about yourself, however. You might instead notice that you're using sugar as a kind of self-medication, boosting your dopamine levels after a long, stressful day. You might observe that you are triggered by the end of a meal, by walking every evening into the kitchen to put the dishes into the sink, and then immediately rummaging in the cupboards for dessert. You realize that you've been running through this same habitual routine for years—you can even feel yourself slipping into unconscious autopilot mode, where your body seems to be running on its own track.

In the chapters that follow, we'll look more closely at practical ways to work with the three-step loop, but in this example, even acknowledging the existence of the three steps means you can start to put together a worthwhile strategy to break and replace this habit.

You could remove the trigger by changing up your dinner routine. You could stop keeping snacks in the house. You could also work hard to replace the habit with something else that also releases dopamine and makes you feel good. You could break the loop by simply distracting yourself. Perhaps most importantly, you could endure your sugar cravings with patience, knowing that it's only a matter of time until your brain relinquishes the old routine and grabs hold of the new one.

Takeaways:

- Habits are repeated, learned behaviors, but they have neurochemical and physiological correlates in the brain.
- Your brain possesses the characteristic of plasticity—i.e., neural pathways can be rewired and old habits can be replaced with new ones. This is what makes it possible for us to learn, adapt and change.
- There are three steps to habit formation: the **trigger** which signals the brain to go into "autopilot" mode, the **routine** behavior itself, and the **reward** that follows and reinforces the behavior.
- The above process is mediated by dopamine, which forms the neurochemical basis for our reward system. When dopamine is released, we form memories of what was pleasurable and felt good, so we're more likely to repeat those behaviors.
- Other hormones like serotonin, GABA and norepinephrine modulate the

balance between goal-directed or habit-directed brain modes.

- If we want to change our bad habits, we need to work with our innate brain mechanisms.

- The pleasure principle is a simple but powerful fundamental motivator of all human (and animal!) behavior. It states that humans are motivated to act in ways that reduce pain and suffering and maximize pleasure.

- The pleasure principle is an evolutionary fact that's all about survival, but it also means that we work harder to avoid pain than we do to seek out pleasure. This may explain why it's hard to proactively make positive changes in life, but relatively easy to avoid massively negative habits.

- Emotion trumps all: what we *perceive* as pleasurable is what matters, and this inevitably means we focus on the present, and ignore long-term outcomes and consequences— another reason that permanent behavioral change is difficult.

- To get rid of unwanted bad behaviors and develop healthy new ones, we need to understand what habits are, learn how they form, and work with our inbuilt tendencies to make lasting changes.

Chapter 2. Habit Formation Psychology

When it comes to habits, it would seem that the physiological, the psychological and the behavioral are all connected, one influencing the other.

When you engage in a habit, your brain fills with neurotransmitters that help you to remember and repeat that action (physical aspect); you experience a strong psychological pull toward the activity from the conditioned cues and triggers these brain chemicals have helped ingrain (psychological aspect); and outwardly your behavior manifests as the habitual routine itself (behavioral aspect).

In this chapter, we'll take a closer look at the psychological aspect of this trio. It's important to note that this is just one lens that we can use to look at habits. One way of thinking about it is to see psychology as our subjective experience of our physiological and neurochemical reality. We've seen what habits look like in the brain, now let's look at how they express themselves in our lived experience. More importantly, how can we use this information to motivate ourselves to form good habits, and undo bad ones?

Habit formation from a psychological perspective

In the last chapter we saw that **habits are essentially automated, repeated, unconscious behaviors we engage in without thinking about them too much**, and that they have a real neurochemical basis in our brains. By understanding how and why habits are formed *physiologically*, we learn how the process works from the inside out. The same can be said for understanding how we form and break habits *psychologically*: the more we understand the process, the better our chances of making lasting changes, from the outside in.

You've probably heard that it takes X number of days to form a new habit, with the number varying from thirty to ninety days or so. One study by Phillippa Lally and her team published in the *European Journal of Social Psychology* put the rough average at around sixty-six days, although there is enormous variation and it depends on the habit one is trying to form.

Lally and colleagues worked with a familiar definition of habits, explaining that when we've done something repeatedly in the past, the repetition over time creates mental associations linking the trigger and the behavior, so that the next time the trigger is encountered, it cues the habit automatically. This is the three-part habit loop we briefly explored in the previous chapter. So, there are two crucial things needed for a habit to form:

- The behavior needs to be repeated regularly (not necessarily daily, but often) and it needs to be uniform, i.e. done the same way every time.

- There needs to be an association between the trigger or specific environment and the resulting behavior.

So, if you're in a particular situation or environment, your previous history will trigger you to automatically perform behaviors you've done before, without thinking about it. This is key—it's the difference between forcing yourself through a workout you hate, and simply going to the gym because it's something you always do in the mornings, like brushing your teeth. You could theoretically perform an action every day but, until it is done *consistently and automatically in response to a trigger*, it's not really a habit, it's just something you've managed to force yourself to do repeatedly.

If we hope to make new habits, we need to make sure we're mimicking the natural process of habit formation, and designing precisely the situations that will lead a habit to form. Many people take up new exercise or diet routines, or they may try to start a habit like reading every day, or develop a new skill such as playing an instrument. But until these activities become both regular and completely automatic, they're not habits.

As you already know, willpower is expensive, cognitively speaking. It requires a large energy output and is not sustainable. But our goal with this book is to take productive, healthy behaviors and make them habitual, so they are sustainable. In other words, we do all the right things automatically when triggered by our environment, do them regularly, and do them without thought.

Just think about that for a moment: imagine that all the behaviors associated with excellence and success come to you automatically and without you having to think to yourself every time, "Ah, I have to force myself to practice violin today." Imagine simply doing all these things with the same amount of mental effort it takes to have a shower or eat dinner at night.

Not understanding what a habit actually is means people often fail to develop them properly. You could force yourself to do this or that, but these activities in themselves may not mean much in the bigger picture. Understanding that there are three steps to the process—trigger, routine and reward—means you can set to work *creating the conditions for the habit to form*, rather than constantly wrestling with the activity itself.

So, to build habits, we need to create the environment that triggers those habits.

If you look closely, you'll see that all the habits you hold right now were formed in this way. Think of anything you do routinely every day, and there's a strong chance that behavior didn't become fixed because you simply decided one day it was what you were going to do. The three-step loop ran on its own, and the habit you have now is the result.

In fact, it's impossible *not* to form habits, and you will do so without trying, as you already have with so many of your current habits. But our goal is to consciously control the process of habit formation so we can direct and shape the behaviors we most want to make part of our lives.

Remember that habits form for a reason—they are your brain's attempt to decrease mental load and put predictable and already-mastered tasks on the back burner so you can focus on the more "cognitively expensive" novel tasks. What does this tell us? That having a habit is easy, but making one from scratch is hard. Like riding a bike, it's challenging at first and requires your full, goal-directed higher mind (your prefrontal cortex). But afterwards, you can do it literally without thinking, as your basal ganglia or habit brain takes over for you.

You might have felt really scared and stressed out by learning to ride a bike as a kid, and may have even decided you didn't like it. But once it became easier and routine, you actually did start to enjoy it, and may even choose to ride a bike now just for pleasure. What this tells us is that a habit can be pleasurable, even though the activity might not be pleasurable to start off with.

Are you beginning to see why it's so hard (but so necessary) to set up new habits?

So long as we are consciously working at developing a new behavior (maybe for sixty-six days, maybe for longer), it will be one thing only: hard work. But after that, we gain a little mastery, we become familiar with the routine, and our three-step habit loop has had the chance to cement the behavior with a reward courtesy of your neurotransmitter friend, dopamine. After this point, it's easier to do the habit than it is to not do it. Success!

Though this seems like an almost ridiculously simple mechanism, the truth is that understanding how habits work and how to form good ones is perhaps the most useful thing you can learn in life. For a start, good habits help you to learn. A habit carries you through the dull and boring parts of a process—any process. A habit helps you overcome defeat, failure, uncertainty or fatigue. You just keep going. Habit makes you resilient.

With habits, you make constant, incremental steps toward your goals, and more than this, you slowly develop your character and self-esteem. What is a person except the sum of all the things they do, day in and day out? When we talk about admirable qualities like leadership, creativity or dedication, aren't we really talking about the consistent repeated *actions* we associate with these traits?

If we rely on simple instinct and pleasure in the moment, we don't get very far. If we give up at the first challenge, we never progress along life's paths, we don't learn or grow, we don't evolve out of our comfort zones. Daily habits are the mechanism that allow us to reach our dreams; a habit is like the vehicle that takes you where you want to go, one mile at a time. And if you are committing beneficial actions to automatic habit, you're doing something else: freeing up your higher brain to learn even more, and develop further.

Mastering the formation of good habits is not just for practical matters like eating healthier; it's also for psychological growth like changing negative self-talk or habits of self-criticism. By changing your behavior toward yourself, you ultimately influence your own internal models of who you are, your self-esteem, and sense of identity. This leads to better choices and a stronger conscious will, reinforcing a "virtuous cycle" that fosters greater development and achievement with time.

Making and breaking habits

A curious thing about habits is that, even though the overall mechanism is designed to help your brain, individual habits can actually be incredibly harmful. Most of our habits save enormous amounts of time (can you imagine having to learn how to put on your shoes every single morning from scratch?) and give us enormous freedom and flexibility to "bank" certain skills and move on.

But the three-stage loop of trigger-behavior-reward is prone to interference. When the dopamine reward system in the brain is dysregulated, people may find themselves addicted, repeatedly performing certain actions for what seems like diminishing dopamine rewards. And since the process of habit formation relies so heavily on repetition of what worked in the past, some of your most stubborn habits could well have been formed in childhood, when you didn't have much of a say over the conditions or the rewards associated with certain behaviors.

Though some habits are very simple, acquired early in life and near instinctual (like washing yourself or eating something for breakfast), others are more complex and required a little more initial effort and "programming" (like driving a car, speaking a language or playing an instrument). Habits can be "good" or "bad," but this doesn't mean that good habits are mentally more work to maintain—some people may go for a daily jog as easily as they breathe air, and others may take several attempts at smoking before they derive any pleasure from it.

Whatever your bad habit is (too much screen time, smoking, drinking, overeating or staying up too late at night), you can derive some comfort from knowing that the same mechanisms that hold that habit in place could just as easily support healthier, better habits. The mental load is the same, with the exception of the initial adjustment period.

We are dwelling on the anatomy of habits, both good and bad, because we cannot begin the process of changing bad ones into good ones until we understand the anatomy of a habit and why it exists. It's not a question of wanting it badly enough, or being a good person, or having enough willpower. Rather, it's about skillfully working with your own motivations and unconscious mental processes to design habits the way you want them, in order to support the kind of life you want.

Let's look at what a good habit brings to your life: your days run more smoothly, and with less time and mental energy spent on everyday activities, so you don't get as tired. There is no force or "discipline" needed—you just do it. With many habits, you become quicker and more efficient with time, too. You save your higher order mental faculties like problem solving and creativity for more important things.

Sounds good so far. But there are downsides to having habits, *both good and bad.*

Bad habits can have us feeling like slaves with no free will, and can actively harm our mental and physical health, eroding our self-esteem and possibly even damaging relationships with others and our work. We become trapped in an endless loop we can't escape, and big chunks of our lives lose dynamism and energy, and become mechanical instead.

However, this mechanical nature is not reserved for bad habits only. Even good habits have their drawbacks. While we feel stable and secure in ourselves when we are running along our routines, we simultaneously narrow our scope for more conscious and creative thinking. We shut ourselves off from learning anything new— after all, why would we? Our brain is already convinced everything is just fine as it is.

Entrenched habits also make us less flexible and able to adapt to change. We are more easily disturbed if our routine is interrupted, and less able to think on our feet and respond spontaneously (as though we've been sleepwalking, which in a way we have!). Our habits don't need to be bad to create tension with others, or to make us behave in stubborn and inflexible ways. All the more reason to know exactly how to change a habit when it's no longer working.

First, we need to understand the different habit types.

Habit typology

For our purposes, let's divide habits into three general classes:

Motor habits

These are all the habits we develop to help us perform physical, muscular activities needed in everyday life. This includes things like standing, walking and running, sitting, holding your body in certain postures, balancing, jumping, and doing exercises that require the coordinated action of different muscles.

Intellectual habits

These are habits concerning one's inner cognitive and mental processes, including activities like perception, analyzing data, constructing logical arguments, using language and rational thought, asking questions, testing hypotheses, arriving at conclusions and so on. In ordinary life, this may be as simple as balancing your budget at the end of the month or fixing a lawnmower, and as complex as earning a degree or planning a political campaign.

Character habits

These are the more psychological expressions of our own personalities, values and principles. Habits and character mutually define and strengthen one another—good habits entrench good character over time, and vice versa. Character habits are those things that allow us to behave in certain ways in the world, more in terms of a *how* than a *what*.

Being honest and hardworking, always saying thank you and practicing gratitude, being a good listener, having good grooming habits and keeping a tidy home, developing good time management, learning to write and speak well, and staying informed and up to date are all habits that achieve more than their immediate purpose; they also express our inner character and communicate our values to others. In time, good character habits cultivate positive emotions and strong self-esteem, giving us enormous psychological satisfaction.

Most people focus on intellectual and character habits, and those daily routines that are a mix of all three. On closer inspection, you might discover that a habit you're trying to either make or break is actually made up of several smaller habits—it's important to note this as it will make a difference to our approach going forward.

The father of behavioral psychology William James famously had a few "rules" for effectively forming new habits, using much of the information we've considered so far. He believed that firstly, you need to make a good start, with plenty of enthusiasm and motivation at the outset and no wavering intention or uncertainty. This energy carries you through the difficult initial patches. Just begin, and go for it. Start quickly and don't delay.

His next suggestion was an obvious one: keep going. Because a key feature of a habit is that you do it over and over again, you need to cement the behavior in your mind by practicing it continually. Keep procrastination and distraction to a minimum, especially in the first few weeks where the new habit is still not firmly established. Keep going, no matter what— no excuses.

Next, make sure that your environment is supporting you. Surround yourself with people who understand your mission and won't interrupt or distract you. Eliminate triggers for bad behaviors and if you can, start your new routine on a clean page, somewhere novel, where you can begin afresh far from the influence of old triggers.

Make sure that you are rewarding yourself somehow every time you perform the good habit.

Finally, you don't stop—even when the behavior is rooted into your routine. That's because the more you practice, the stronger that habit will get, and the less likely you are to relapse.

Laying it all out like that, one could be forgiven for thinking that William James might have oversimplified things. If it's this easy to create a new habit, then why don't people do it more often? A paper in the *Journal of Clinical Psychology* found that more than half (54 percent) of people who tried to make a positive change couldn't keep it going past six months, and that on average, a person makes the same attempt to change *ten times* in the course of their lives. Clearly, there's something else going on.

So, let's ask another question: what is preventing us from forming new, better habits?

New habits—where we go wrong

For the most part, nobody questions why behavioral change is necessary.

Most people can immediately list the benefits of having a healthy diet, exercising, quitting smoking, improving relationship communication, or any other positive personal adjustments we can make. And those who can't answer offhand can find out easily from family, friends, and the more reputable sites on the Internet. We know, logically, why change is good. We know staying the course is detrimental and has a host of negative consequences. We know staying still is the same as continuing on the harmful path.

So why don't we make changes?

Well, it's always easier said than done. It's one thing to understand the benefit of change from an intellectual standpoint; it's quite another to put it into action. Knowing doesn't replace doing. But why isn't just *knowing* why we should do something enough to *motivate* us?

As wonderful a tool as the brain is, we're actually driven by a lot of factors that have little to do with logic. In fact, you can argue that logic is far, far down on the list of factors that influence our daily actions. Evolutionarily, this means logic probably wasn't a big reason our species survived. We may have the inspiration, sustained interest, and determination—but there are other forces, both internal and external, that keep us from effecting meaningful change.

It's now well documented how harmful smoking can be to one's health. The science is long-established and fairly ironclad. Nobody will tell you smoking's good for you, not even cigarette manufacturers, who are legally required to tell you that it contributes to death and various ailments. But many can't quit because their addiction to nicotine is too strong, and they fear the physical discomfort of withdrawal that will come if they stop smoking. Their logical brains know the benefits; their illogical bodies couldn't care less. Their illogical bodies just want to seek pleasure and to avoid pain.

These illogical obstacles to behavior change come from many directions, so it's helpful to organize them into three realms: *conscious, subconscious, and external factors*. These three categories accurately represent our thought processes in daily life. We are conscious of many of our own limitations, yet we don't consciously realize all that is holding us back, and sometimes we can't help but fall prey to an outside influence.

Conscious Psychological Factors

Some of our negative reactions to the idea of changing come from places we're well aware of. They're preexistent problems we consciously know we're dealing with. They're attitudes about ourselves that, given a little prodding, we might readily admit we possess. Although overcoming these self-thoughts is difficult, it's not impossible. In fact, they're far easier to diagnose and treat than the subconscious factors we'll cover next. But our conscious obstructions are equally as important to watch and hopefully reduce as much as possible. These limitations include:

Low self-esteem and confidence. *"I just can't do it. I'm not strong or disciplined enough."*

Maybe the most common internal factor is the feeling that we just can't do it. We're not good, strong, smart, or agile enough to get it done. Often we compare ourselves to other people who seem to do what we want to achieve quite easily, and we know we'll never measure up to their abilities. We'll never be as good as that actor, that singer, that motivational speaker, that politician, or even that friend of ours who seems to handle everything beautifully. We make all these unfair comparisons, while we forget that at one time these others' level of expertise was exactly what ours is now— not much.

Negative self-image. *"I'm just not the type of person to do this. I never will be."*

This is similar to low self-esteem but may be even more destructive and tragic. More than just feeling that we can't do something, negative self-image is thinking that we don't even *deserve* to. All possibilities of change and action are closed to us because we're not worthy. This strain of thought is more dangerous than low self-esteem because it implies that we're condemned to an unfulfilling life, so even attempting to change ourselves is a waste of time. A person with low self-esteem might still believe they're at least *entitled* to a better existence, but someone with a negative self-image doesn't believe they merit any kind of positivity at all. "I don't deserve a happy relationship because I've been doomed all my life" or "I don't deserve to be successful at work—that level of prosperity is only for people better than me."

Over-tolerance of pain or discomfort. *"I might be coughing all the time from smoking too much, but the withdrawal would be way worse."*

Endurance and strength during times of hardship are good traits, but if unchecked they can obscure realities about our situations. If we suffer injury, tribulation, or distress merely because we have faith that things will eventually get better, we could be promoting inaction. The current situation might be awful, but trying to do something about it might make it even worse. So nothing is done—and nothing changes. This can also be disguised as simple denial and refusing to admit the intensity of pain or discomfort to avoid taking action.

Confrontation avoidance. *"I don't know. I don't want to upset them and make it awkward."*

The act of change almost inevitably entails some sort of conflict. Certainly you'll experience tension with yourself, against some of your oldest and ugliest truths. But you might also clash with other people who aren't tuned in to the change you're undergoing or who might be opposed or uncooperative about it. Rather than deal with these kinds of confrontations in a constructive way, one might be more inclined to retreat into a familiar bubble and avoid the possibility of facing the consequences: "This Buddhist meditation class might make my ultra-religious mother upset."

Fear of failure or rejection. *"Everyone's going to laugh at my painting anyway, so I'm not going to take that art class."*

Every single attempt to bring about change runs the risk of disappointment. But for some, the possibility of failure is a terrifying concept: it reinforces their worst fears about their abilities or lack thereof and drives them to the belief that they're better off not even trying. Similarly, the often-exaggerated fear of being dismissed or criticized by other people can immobilize one's efforts to change. They might, therefore, reject the proposed change preemptively—before they suffer rejection themselves. Their current level of suffering is a walk in the park compared to confirming how incapable or untalented they are.

Subconscious Psychological Factors

If they're not immediately recognizable, conscious attitudes are at least well known enough that we can identify them somewhat quickly. Not so with subconscious factors.

These forces operate without our knowledge; we don't perceive that they're negatively affecting our drive to change (or that they even exist). They are extremely potent at eroding our self-attitudes and often recur in our lives over a very long period of time, to the extent that they derail our entire life story. These are the automatic negative thoughts and beliefs that cognitive behavioral therapy seeks to exorcise.

Many of these subconscious factors share common points with the conscious ones we've just discussed. But the subconscious factors can be more dangerous because they've been chipping away at our identities relatively undetected—and are therefore more strongly woven into our beings. They're working on us under the total cover of darkness, so it's harder to call them up and deal with them head-on.

Limiting beliefs and narratives. *"That's impossible for me. I've never been that type of person."*

These are similar to the conscious negativity generated by low self-esteem and poor self-image—but these beliefs are ingrained in us when we're young and become part of ourselves without our knowing. With limiting self-narratives, you are locked into a narrow view of what you can do or what's *proper* for you to do. You see life through a lens of pessimism and doubt. You mistrust good fortune or positivity. You're obsessed with catastrophe and dismissive of happiness.

And if a certain story doesn't fit into your oppositional point of view, you'll *make* it fit: "I'm not going for that promotion because that level of success turns people into jerks" or "Falling in love and intimacy are overrated, inconvenient, and usually very expensive—I got no time for that." This is the story you keep telling yourself, about yourself, couched in negative undertones. You've done it for so long it has become a part of your identity, for better or worse. You literally cannot think in a different manner, and your worldview is skewed in a unique and detrimental way.

Fixed mindset. *"It's just not something I'll ever improve at. I'm destined to be bad forever."*

This is a twist on the self-identity factors, originally introduced by Stanford psychologist Carol Dweck. The fixed mindset declares that the traits we have are permanent and unchangeable. Our intelligence, temperament, personality, and creative talent cannot be significantly altered. Therefore, the fixed mindset defines success as how well our traits stack up against those of others, usually in a quantitative way. Since those traits can never be altered or improved according to a fixed mindset, we can only triumph by proving our traits are superior to others'. A person with a fixed mindset fears failure, perceiving it as evidence that we're stupid, untalented, or lacking in character—things that can't be changed.

"Growth mindsets," though, are oriented toward the tenet that personal traits are malleable and can always be improved upon: you *can* increase your intelligence, you *can* learn and develop a talent, you *can* make adjustments to your personality. Therefore, the growth mindset embraces challenges, seeing failure as a learning opportunity and a pivot toward expanding ourselves—*not* proof of unintelligence or inability.

These mindsets can be implanted in us at a critically young age, and they hold the keys to our behaviors and attitudes toward success and failure in everything, professionally and personally speaking. They therefore have a direct impact on our faculties for satisfaction and happiness.

A fixed mindset would say, "This job requires skills I'm terrible at and will never get better at," whereas a growth mindset would say, "This job looks challenging—*and I can't wait to get started on it!*"

Past experience or trauma. *"I don't know. It went terribly once before so it probably will be again this time."*

What we've gone through in the past has an ongoing and direct impact on how we approach or avoid certain situations later in life. While that may seem like an obvious statement few would disagree with, in practice the influence happens without our discerning it.

Most of our responses to such stimuli—and indeed, the stimuli themselves—stem from our subconscious. We don't understand why we have such aversion or disgust toward certain things or what led to those negative feelings in the first place. It then follows quite easily into our refusing to change our existent behavior or shunning unfamiliar ones. Someone might be scared of romantic commitments because their parents seemed terminally unhappy or abusive to each other. They might not want to learn to drive because they were involved in a car wreck as a child.

External Environmental Factors

This third plank of avoidance in changing behavior is significant enough that it deserves its own chapter—so I'll give it one later in this book. But I'm also briefly mentioning them here because these environmental barriers "work" side by side with the internal forces preventing us from changing our behaviors. It is notable to mention that some of these are legitimate, while others are rationalizations to avoid taking action.

Lack of practical knowledge or education. *"I don't even know what I don't know."*

Simply put, you don't have (or don't think you have) sufficient instruction, training, or information to pursue the change you want. Alternately, you can't find any way to get that kind of knowledge, even in the age of super-information. "I can't even boil water—how am I going to learn how to cook Indian food?" "I can't afford that transcendental meditation class, so I might as well forget about it."

Of course, information has never been easier to find than it is today—if anything, there is too much information available, which would cause analysis paralysis. Yet still, some people don't know where to start.

Too many obligations. *"I'm way too busy for that. I work and have seven kids and eight dogs."*

Adult responsibilities have this way of piling up to the point of overload: family, partners, children, work, home maintenance, car maintenance, bills—take your pick. This not only affects your schedule for working on change, but also could just drain you so much that you're not even aware of the changes you need to make. "Yeah, between driving the kids to school and soccer class, finishing this work project, getting the roof gutter fixed, remembering my sister's birthday, and cleaning out the refrigerator—sure, I'll start working out."

This can indeed be a real concern and barrier, but often it comes with an overestimation of how much time is necessary to really begin to change behavior. It's not difficult to carve out fifteen minutes every day, but easier said than done.

Big fish, small pond. *"I'm good here. Don't worry about it."*

If you're already doing well in your current environment, if you're operating at a level above other people in your immediate view—isn't that "good enough"? You're so much better than everyone else in your surroundings that you don't understand why you need to improve. You're happy in your echo chamber, where nobody disagrees or offers you criticism, so as far as you're concerned, you're doing fine. "Why do I have to address my gambling problem? I beat every other guy in this town at Texas hold 'em!"

Plainly put, you are too comfortable or too insulated from negative consequences. This is not a bad thing, but it certainly doesn't make you hungry for change.

Harmful or opposing environment. *"He doesn't stop talking to me, so I can never get into a groove."*

Sometimes circumstances or settings have a damaging or highly uncomfortable effect on our natures, or they don't have the elements we require to start a program of change. A very introverted person might not be able to operate well in a crowded or loud place, or a person living in a very conservative community might feel discouraged about studying outside cultures. There are many ways our direct environments can impact us, and you'll read about them later.

Social inertia or rejection. *"No one else is doing it... and they might laugh at me and think I'm stupid!"*

This is an external manifestation of the confrontational avoidance and fear of rejection that we discussed above—however, we should also allow for the possibility that you're *not* merely paranoid. You very well may be part of a social scene where people you see every day are profoundly disinterested in who you are or what you try to do and, in fact, are pretty much slackers themselves who are resistant to change on a group level. They have no interest themselves in change and actively drag you down to their level, belittling any effort or caring on your part. That's social inertia.

Fears of rejection, on the other hand, might stem from worries that your change will disrupt the social order around you to the point where you're treated as an outcast. "If I start an exercise program, everybody I hang out with at the sports bar is going to tease me or think I'm working too hard." (Although if that's how they really think, you may just need to find better friends.)

So anyone who's thinking about making a change in their lives is not at a loss for opposing forces, within or outside themselves. All of these forces—even the ones we don't notice or comprehend—can be conquered. It may look like a very tall order at the outset, but it's absolutely achievable. Understanding the obstacles is an important part of the battle. A doctor wouldn't operate without a clear understanding of what to remove, and attempting to forge ahead with behavioral change without first introspecting is similarly foolhardy.

Getting started is usually the most overwhelming part of the change process, and it depends on the strength and clarity of our motivation. That's what we'll address next.

Takeaways:

- Forming new habits has a physiological, psychological and a behavioral component. By understanding the psychology of the way habits are made and broken, we can work to create better ones.

- A behavior needs to be uniform, repeated regularly, and must automatically follow a trigger in the environment. It takes no conscious effort. Establishing behaviors may be difficult to begin with, but becomes easier with time; likewise they may not be enjoyable at first, but can become more so with time.

- By understanding the three-step loop of habit formation, we can create the environment needed to support new habits, while discouraging old ones.

- There are different types of habits, and they can each have both advantages and disadvantages, whether they're "good" or "bad."

- Even though we logically and intellectually know what we should do, why don't do we those things? Because despite what we like to think, we aren't really operating on conscious free will most of the time. There are three categories of obstacles to doing what we truly want at any point: *conscious, subconscious,* and *external* factors.

- Conscious factors are ones we know and readily tell ourselves. They are what we repeat when we fail or decide not to do something. They include low self-esteem, negative self-image, over-tolerance of pain or discomfort, aversion to confrontation, and fear of failure and rejection.

- Subconscious factors are similar to the conscious factors, yet they are so deeply ingrained in our identities we don't even realize we hold these beliefs—they are just our automatic thought patterns. They include limiting beliefs and narratives, having a fixed mindset, and being victim to traumatic experiences.

- External factors are outside of ourselves. They are the environmental or social pressures that keep us from taking action. Some of these are legitimate; some are simply excuses. These include lack of knowledge, too many obligations, being too comfortable, harmful environments, social inertia, or rejection.

Chapter 3. The Framework for Lasting Change

In the previous chapter, we took a close look at what a habit actually is, the kinds of habits that fill our days and how exactly habits form, from a behavioral perspective but also neurochemically. We also looked at the psychological aspect behind habit formation and why it can be so hard to break bad habits and form better ones. In this chapter, we'll be bringing all of this together to answer the question you're probably most interested in: how can you *change* your habits... permanently?

It all comes back to neuroplasticity, and knowing how to use it to our advantage. We've laid the groundwork and now it's time to examine the ways we can work with the processes that are already underway within our own brains. This bears repeating: every day, in every moment, you already possess countless habits, whether you are conscious of them or not.

Forming habits is the easiest thing in the world—you've done it all your life without thinking. But consciously developing the habits that you deliberately choose is another story. Once you understand the underlying principles in this chapter, you'll be able to apply them to a range of contexts, habits and goals.

Good or bad—it's all the same to the brain

You might have already noticed this: in our earlier discussion on the three steps behind habit formation, we didn't specify whether the habits were good or bad, healthy or unhealthy, productive or unproductive.

That's because **to your brain, a habit is just a habit**. The brain's main goal in forming a habit is to conserve cognitive energy—there's no moral element. Rather, creating habits is a natural part of the human mental experience, and is as value neutral as the act of breathing or digesting food.

Your unconscious, automatic mind cannot tell the difference between good and bad habits. It knows which actions are *easiest* to do (i.e. the ones that have seemed to work before) but it's not really concerned whether those actions are jeopardizing your future, or making you unhappy in the long run.

The good news is that your *conscious* mind does know all these things. Our higher minds can and do distinguish between habits that bring us closer to our goals and those that undermine us. It's probably this higher, more conscious part of you that led you to read this book in the first place—you knew on some level that your current habits weren't working anymore.

The entire self-help industry is built around the idea that we can and should change our behavior. That if only we want it badly enough, we can break our old habits and be better, quit addictions, lose weight, make more money, or whatever else. But the truth is that your habits, helpful as your brain might think they are, are the very thing standing in your way of changing.

Think about it: habits and change directly oppose one another. If it feels like a fight to change your old ways, that's because it is—it's a battle between ingrained, entrenched and fixed ways of doing things and the enormous energy it takes to step out and do something different.

The trouble with the ordinary approach is that we think about change at the higher, conscious level but never really access our deeper, unconscious level. This is why you can know that a habit is bad for you but keep on doing it anyway. Where it counts, you don't really *know*. Willpower doesn't matter, force doesn't matter—you can only change a habit when you work at the level at which habits are created.

Defining a good habit is simple: it's any habit that has a positive effect on your overall life goals, health or well-being. A bad habit is the inverse: anything that actively works against your overall life goals, health and well-being.

A good habit has concrete, cumulative benefits in your life. Brushing your teeth means you don't get cavities, studying a little each day means you're prepared for the test, investing a small amount per month means you accrue savings. Bad habits work the other way, taking you further from the goals you've set for yourself, or working to undermine your general health and wellness. Every cigarette you smoke, every workout you skip, every sugar binge, every time you chew your nails, every moment you spend listening to negative self-talk... All these things work to chip away at the good things in life.

That's the sneaky thing about habits: the effects may seem negligible in the day to day, but they compound over time. Eating three donuts one day doesn't really matter, but eating three donuts *every* day, for years on end, will absolutely have a negative effect.

You might ask, what about those habits that are somewhere in the middle, the neutral ones that don't take you closer or further from your goals, but just keep you where you are? Naturally, if they save mental effort, and they *genuinely* make little difference otherwise, it doesn't matter. But if we're honest, many of the habits we think are harmless actually do cost us in the long run.

For example, a common way for bad habits to have their effect is indirectly, via the opportunity cost. This is everything we miss out on because we were clinging to a particular habit, so that essentially it hogs the spot that could have gone to a habit that actually makes your life better. You could be in the habit of eating certain things over and over again, and miss out on discovering a new favorite food that's also a source of nutrients you don't often get. Yes, being a picky eater is more or less a harmless habit, but why bother to maintain it if it doesn't improve your life in any way?

How to create a habit

So, if sheer willpower or wishful thinking isn't effective, what is? Let's take a closer look, and we'll start with one task in particular: how to create *new* habits, from scratch.

Let's look again at the trigger-routine-reward loop behind new habit formation. We'll consider a range of different behavioral techniques, but before we do that, we need to know what habits we'd like to actually develop. A great exercise is to take a piece of paper and divide it into three columns, each labeled "trigger," "routine" and "reward." First, choose around five new habits that you'd like to develop, based on your goals and interests.

This shouldn't be too hard. If you're unhappy with your fitness levels, for example, you could identify the goal of being a better runner, and decide on the habit of running for twenty minutes every morning. If your goal is to have a great holiday at the end of the year, you might set a habit of saving a fixed amount every month.

The next step is to identify triggers that will cue you to perform this new habit. A good idea is to "piggyback" new habits onto old ones. If you already brush your teeth every day, without fail, then tack on the new habit of going for a run on top of this habit, so you're reminded to put your running shoes on every time you finish brushing your teeth in the morning. If you do your online banking every Sunday evening, take that as your trigger to set something aside in a special savings pot.

Finally, the reward column. Now, you need to be clever about this—you don't want to be indirectly creating new bad habits! Simply plan something to do immediately after you've performed the desired habit that will cement it, and tell your brain "do this again" in the language it understands: dopamine.

You could withhold having your much-loved first cup of coffee for the day until after you've finished your jog. Or you could give yourself a few minutes to daydream about the holiday you'll have every week after you diligently put some money into the pot. It doesn't matter what you do, really, only that your brain genuinely perceives it as pleasurable.

Take the time to really pause and relish the reward. Wring out every drop of dopamine from the experience you can! Many people find that simply feeling proud of their achievements is enough of a reward. They track their progress visually using a chart, for example, and get a little thrill every time they cross something off the list or put another gold sticker on the poster. This is a very healthy way to reward yourself, since you are deriving pleasure from the act itself, reinforcing for your brain that this is something you like and enjoy, and want to keep doing.

If you take the time to plan it carefully, your reward for one behavior can actually serve double duty as the trigger for another. You could dive into your delicious cup of coffee, and when you're done, this signals to you that you should take your vitamins. Before you know it, your day could potentially be one long conveyor belt of healthy habits triggering more healthy habits—the opposite of that downward spiral of bad behaviors that seem to feed off one another.

Not only does this simple technique make it more likely that you'll stick through the transition period and make your new habits concrete, it also just feels good. You won't be forcing and pushing yourself and feeling miserable, but instead scheduling in many little dopamine bubbles throughout the day. Your energy levels will be more even and consistent, and you'll reach that stage we all want to be in—that feeling of actually looking forward to what's good for you, enjoying it, then feeling proud and satisfied after you've done it.

Habits don't have to be done daily. You could make your yearly tax return a lot less painful by rewarding yourself with a yearly trip to the spa once it's done, for example. Something to remember, however, is that smaller habit loops are easier to instill than bigger ones. This is because you give your brain more opportunities to reinforce the habit through reward. Knowing this, you could try where possible to break less frequent habits down so they can be done in smaller parts, more often.

Once you've spent some time trying to strengthen a new habit, you can reassess your original list and see if any adjustments are needed. Once a habit is well set, you won't need to continually reward yourself. On the other hand, if the habit just doesn't seem to stick, you might need to rethink the triggers or give yourself a more compelling reward.

Notice that nowhere in this process are you *forcing* yourself or using willpower. You are working only with triggers and rewards, which already form the architecture of habit formation anyway. The three-step loop is simple, but there are countless ways to exploit our understanding of its principles.

A smart way to augment this process is with affirmations. An affirmation is basically a belief you tell yourself again and again until it becomes automatic, until the thought is something you genuinely believe.

Remember that your brain likes repetition. What you do often and regularly starts to feel like what you *should* be doing. In other words, the more you tell your brain something, the more it thinks it must be true.

So, when you wake up, then brush your teeth, immediately say the affirmation, "I can't wait for my run. I love running," and then go do it. Sounds silly, but you *will* start to believe it after a while. Mental habits, beliefs and perceptions often precede outward behavioral changes. But you can also jump-start the process by encouraging your brain to believe it already possesses that habit.

Another way to internalize the three-step process is to use if-then statements, which capture the essence of trigger and reward. For example, *if* I keep practicing salsa every day, *then* I'll get really good at it and feel fantastic. In the morning, you could tell yourself, "If I go for my run, my fitness levels will improve, I'll feel good about myself, and hey, I'll get to enjoy my nice cup of coffee afterwards." We'll look at this technique in more detail later.

Understanding the architecture of a habit, we can get to work building them for ourselves. The idea is to establish the conditions you know will automatically activate certain mental associations and trigger a learnt response that has been conditioned through repetition (and dopamine!). Using just the right triggers and environmental conditions, you can elicit the behaviors you want until they become automatic, removing the need for volition and effort and making the right behavior effortless and spontaneous.

No matter how disciplined or motivated you are, ingrained habits are typically stronger. To change behavior for good, we need to rework our habits—*not* focus more on our motivation or willpower. The happy truth is that you can make significant and lasting changes to your life even if you're a little lazy, or unmotivated, or have already failed a few times before.

In the world of behavior change and self-improvement, you can see the distinction between those techniques that take your compliance as granted, and those that understand nothing will really change until you make it habitual. It's a shift in perspective and a reframing of goals; it's the difference between "it would be nice to have a six-pack" and "I am making concrete efforts to develop the habit of doing crunches every single day."

Many different schools of thought have independently arrived at different techniques that, on closer inspection, are actually just variations of the three-step process we've outlined above. Whether it's to curb impulsive spending, eat better, exercise, quit a harmful addiction, practice a skill or follow through on healthy lifestyle behaviors, **what seems to work again and again is one thing: context-dependent repetition, followed by reinforcing reward.**

A 2008 paper in the *International Journal of Obesity* by Lally and colleagues investigated whether habit formation was any better at helping participants maintain healthier lifestyles compared to non-habit methods.

The research found that those using routinization, identifying cues, habit substitution and self-monitoring lost more weight than those who didn't, and they kept it off. Interestingly, habits only seemed to strengthen the longer the participants kept up their program.

In the same vein, a 2017 paper by Kaushal and colleagues in the *British Journal of Health Psychology* showed that when people were trained on how to set up cues for themselves, how to increase their enjoyment of certain activities, and how to strengthen and reinforce good habits, they showed more physical activity when compared to a control group. A 2014 paper by Pedersen et al used a similar approach to get office workers to spend less time sitting and more time being physically active.

There are countless similar papers showing similar results—when behavioral change is made *habitual*, it sticks. So, what exactly are all the techniques used in these dozens of studies? What they all have in common is that they exploit the way the brain naturally works. Though there's tons of advice out there, the truth is that it's difficult to pinpoint a single technique or method that will work 100 percent for your unique life and goals. Nevertheless, a thorough 2019 review article by Gardner and Rebar looked at what most behavioral interventions have in common, and they found a few key factors that made the biggest difference:

1. **Consistently repeat behavior in the same context**. Repetition is important, but it needs to be done in the same environment every time so your brain can make associations that can be reliably triggered the next time round. For example, putting important medicine near the bathroom sink and taking it every morning when you brush your teeth—the same habit is paired with the same bathroom sink, day in and day out. This aspect is by far the most powerful way to cement new habits (it also tells us something interesting about how to *break* habits—which we'll cover in the next section...)

2. **Build in cues and prompts**. Even once in the same environment or

context, you need something to trigger a learnt behavioral response. In the above example, it's brushing your teeth. If you go to use that bathroom sink at another time during the day to wash your hands, you won't be triggered to take your medicine again—it's context PLUS trigger that equals behavior. Another example is to use an alarm to trigger you to start work, a nightly cup of herbal tea to trigger winding down for the evening, or getting out of the shower to trigger your daily bathroom tidying routine.

3. **Plan ahead consciously**. Learnt habits are spontaneous and effortless in the moment, but that doesn't mean you can't lay the groundwork ahead of time to make that effortlessness more likely to occur. Planning your actions ahead of time opens up a window for you to consciously choose how you'd like to act, and gives you some control over the environment and the cues that precede and follow the desired habit.

This could be drawing up a three-step chart as explained earlier, or it could simply be a matter of telling yourself, "When I take the train this evening, that's my cue to read a little from my Spanish book."

4. **Set goals and identify milestones to reach them**. What seemed to work so often for people in these studies, no matter what they were trying to improve, was having a clear roadmap for what they were doing, and how. They performed better when they had clear step-by-step instructions for what they needed to do, and when. It makes sense when you think about it. Habits are often linear and procedural; they're about one step following the other. It's much easier to perform a habit when you know all the steps and their order. So, break down your goals into steps and lay them out: first put on your workout outfit, then stretch, then do strength exercises, then cardio, then cooldown, then shower, and so on. If each individual habit can

cue the next in the series, you are well on your way to making the whole choreography seamless and easy. Another side of this is to give yourself the chance to rehearse or practice. It may seem simple and obvious, but coach yourself through the individual steps, piece by piece. Practice a new movement or technique in slow motion first, imprinting it in your mind.

5. **Monitor yourself**. It's good advice: what gets measured, gets better. When you observe your behaviors, you get to see what works and what doesn't. The simple act of tracking your behavior can also serve as a reward—it feels good to track your progress, since you are essentially giving your brain a mini goal to celebrate and feel satisfied with. You confirm to yourself: *This feels good, keep going.*

Gardner and Rebar did find other factors behind the participants' varying success, but the above were the elements *most* responsible for a favorable outcome. Other techniques included physically altering the surrounding environment (adding or taking away triggers or rewards), seeking social support (which is again a form of trigger or reward—or both), focusing on past success, reframing the situation, avoiding exposure to triggers, comparing yourself to others, getting feedback on your behavior, or using graded tasks (i.e. starting out small and then working your way up to the desired habit).

So, given that there are so many different techniques and approaches, how do you go about making a plan for your own behavioral modification? There are no one-size-fits-all solutions. The technique you choose will not only have to work for the particular habit in question, but it will have to work for you as a unique individual. Furthermore, none of these techniques is likely to be enough on their own—to make the maximum impact, it's worth combining them.

Make sure you're addressing each stage in the three-step loop. You need to build a trigger or cue into the environment (step one), you need to establish a clearly outlined and repeatable behavior (step two), and you need a reward or reinforcer to cement the behavior (step three). In other words, you are supporting new habit formation at the beginning, middle and end of the process.

Let's say you wanted to build a new habit of eating more fruits and vegetables every day. You could identify a clear and specific goal: to eat at least five portions of fruit and veggies per day, one for breakfast and two each for lunch and dinner. Then, you'd consider the first part of the process, the trigger or cue. You could make some changes to your environment, like placing fruit on your desk, and ensuring you always have ready-prepared servings of salad in the fridge.

For breakfast, you could start by making sure you have a banana with your oatmeal every day. You put the bananas right next to the oats, so that the association is clear— whenever you have oatmeal, you also have a banana. Every day. You establish similar cues for other meals in the day, for example having frozen vegetables on hand when you cook in the evening, and replacing sweets and chocolate with fruit for dessert.

For step two, you could find ways to make it easier on yourself to actually perform the habit. You might support your new habit by augmenting it with positive affirmations and self-praise every time you get it right. You could keep reminding yourself of why you want this habit in the first place by using if-then statements like, "If I keep eating well, I'll be healthier and happier." You could also seek the support of those around you, or plan the next day's meals the night before, so you don't have the chance to succumb to unhealthy temptations.

For the last step, you can think about rewards and incentives. Tell yourself that if you can reach your goal for one week, you'll buy yourself a little treat, or focus more on intrinsic motivation by getting the fruits and veggies you most like. If there's something in your daily schedule that you really enjoy, you might withhold giving it to yourself until the end of the day, after you've reached your five-a-day target. Even little things like putting ticks on a chart on the fridge will help, since they give your brain a little dopamine kick.

Now, none of these actions or techniques are all that ground-breaking when laid out this way, but the trick is to consciously put them all together in just the right way. With a little patience, the initial behavioral scaffolding can come down and you will find yourself naturally performing the behaviors that felt difficult just a few months before. In fact, you may find yourself missing and craving your morning banana, and discover that habits formed this way are surprisingly hard to break!

Though it might seem like these habits are too small to really make a difference, their small size is actually a virtue. Small, modest changes are easier to repeat and maintain over the long term, meaning they become habit faster; grand and overambitious actions may be more inspiring initially, but they often represent unrealistic steps that are hard to maintain.

In the chapters that follow, we'll be looking at specific tips, tricks and techniques that you can try in order to improve your own habits and, ultimately, your life. As long as you clearly understand the underlying mechanism of the three-step loop, however, *any* technique could arguably work. On the other hand, when you don't grasp the principles of habit formation and behavior change, even the most scientifically sound and intelligent strategies will not work for you.

To make real and lasting changes using new habits, ask yourself the following questions:

- What are my goals and exactly how do I plan to achieve them, step by step?
- Can I identify the three-step loop in the habit I'd like to form?
- Can I make changes to each of the three steps?

How to change—not break—a habit

In the previous example on how to develop the habit of eating more fruit and vegetables, you might have noticed one of the techniques was to replace an unhealthy habit (dessert after dinner) with a healthier one (having fruit instead). Knowing what we do about triggers, routines and rewards, it makes sense that it's easier to replace a bad habit with a good one than to get rid of it entirely.

It's a little like Indiana Jones carefully replacing the golden idol with a bag of sand—if you're sensible and match the old habit closely with the new one, you can almost seamlessly move from one to the other, without feeling as though you've made a very big or stressful change. Remember, habits are all about what's easiest and quickest. It's always harder to suppress something entirely than to simply reshape what already exists.

As we already saw, the brain doesn't really distinguish between good and bad habits—the machinery is all the same. So, if you can take out some elements of a habit and replace them with others, you are using your automatic, unconscious mind to your advantage, basically making small tweaks to a mental program that you already run without effort.

The only downside to this approach is that you need to actually be aware of the habit you want to alter...easier said than done. First, identify what you are already doing (for example, eating dessert after dinner). Spend a little time investigating the effect of this behavior. You might already know it's not healthy, but you might need to convince yourself of this further by literally tallying up the cost to your mental, physical or emotional well-being.

Ask yourself what good the current habit actually brings. You wouldn't have the habit unless it served you somehow, so it's no use simply saying it has no purpose at all. Identify why it's there and you can find a healthier alternative that fills the same need. For example, dessert after dinner is nice, but the habit may be more about tasting something sweet and just enjoying the ritual of it all—something you can still achieve with the healthier alternative of fruit.

The more closely the new habit resembles the old in terms of how it satisfies needs, the easier it will be to switch and the more chance it has of sticking. Look at the emotions associated with a habit. Do you do certain things for stress relief, nostalgia, distraction? What does the behavior mean to you and when did you first decide it was worth repeating?

When you replace an old habit with a new one, don't just replace the habit itself, but all the triggers and rewards associated with it. For example, alcoholism treatment plans often suggest that when you give up drinking, you need to make sure you're not constantly exposing yourself to the people who trigger you to drink, or else reward you indirectly afterwards.

Finally, keep in mind that habits are three-dimensional—they involve our thoughts, feelings, behaviors and our wider relationships and lifestyles. We cannot alter one part of the puzzle without it impacting the others, and if we hope to make lasting changes, we need to address every aspect of the habit.

Think about the habit of biting your nails. To break the habit, you need to consider not just the three steps, but also the different areas of your life that are involved.

Physical—The habit is made of conditioned physical actions repeated mindlessly, which have a real effect on your body (sore and bloody nails!). Perhaps you paint a bitter-tasting deterrent on your nails to interrupt yourself from automatically nibbling on your nails. This prevents your brain releasing reward neurochemicals every time you bite your nails. Instead, you train yourself to think nail biting = disgusting!

Emotional and psychological—The habit is triggered by stressors in the environment, and acts to reduce anxiety. It was cemented years ago as a coping mechanism and something you associate with feeling out of control. To address this you try and replace the nail-biting with a guided meditation that has you feeling more empowered and in control again.

Behavioral—Noticing that stressful situations cue the nail biting, you try to replace the behavior with a kind of "circuit breaker" behavior, i.e. you immediately sit on your hands when you notice yourself feeling stressed.

You could also look more broadly and ask why the triggers are there in the first place—you could do a lot to get rid of your stress-driven nail-biting habit, but it may be most effective to simply leave the high-pressure job that is causing you to be so anxious in the first place! Similarly, really deeply ingrained habits may need interventions on the scale of moving home, changing jobs or career, leaving relationships or giving your lifestyle a serious reboot. You're still in effect altering the environment to elicit the desired behavior change.

That said, for most of us, small incremental changes that add up are the real secret to transformation and development. No need to go cold turkey, to give yourself pep talks, or to force anything. As a rule, a small change *that you can maintain* is worth more than a big change that you can't. This is the attitude behind the Japanese philosophy of Kaizen—simply, the art of continuous improvement. No, that doesn't mean you gradually work your way up to eating four dozen bananas for breakfast each morning, it simply means that you reframe your perspective away from final goals and toward the little shifts you can make, right here, day after day.

You'll recall that behaviors take time to become habits. The three-step process we're exploring here is mostly about the transition period that bridges the space between where you are now and where you want to be. Eventually, the training wheels come off and the habit runs on its own. But in the meantime? You need patience.

We can exploit the neurological reward system in our brain by giving ourselves rewards, but what about when we mess up and feel bad about it? This is a crucial step in the journey: what we don't want is to pause, dwell on our unhappiness, and cement the negative associations, making it less likely we'll repeat the positive behavior.

You need to tell yourself (and believe) that slipups and failures *are normal*. There will be a learning curve, a transition period, and a sometimes ungraceful adjustment. How you respond to the slipup matters more than the fact of the error. Brush it off and its effect is minimal—just keep going.

Keep reminding yourself that it's not personal. If something isn't working, change it. One mistake doesn't define your journey. But if you can keep going and learn from mistakes, they become an asset to you. Sometimes, people can fail in their plans not because they're too difficult, but because they're afraid of letting go of old habits, old beliefs, old comfort zones. At these points, you need to remind yourself of why you wanted to change, and the cost of *not* changing. As they say, "What got you're here won't get you there."

Takeaways:

- Your brain cannot tell the difference between a healthy or unhealthy habit—habits are habits, and they're formed in exactly the same way.
- We can only change habits when we make the unconscious conscious, and take deliberate control over the automatic processes that lead to habit formation.

- Habits are small but cumulative in their effect—bad habits undermine our health, relationships, and performance while good habits develop good character, success and well-being, fostering a "virtuous cycle" that leads to further good habits.

- To build a good habit, we need to examine the three-step loop in our own behavior and work to make changes at each level.

- Identify a habit that you wish to develop and look closely for possible preceding triggers and the following reward that reinforces it via the dopamine-based reward system.

- Now, build the trigger into your own life, ensuring you're rewarding yourself to cement the habit every time you follow through with the behavior. Keep repeating the same behavior in the same environmental context, and track your progress.

- A new behavior takes time to take root, so you need patience and dedication in the meantime.

- There are dozens of scientifically proven techniques to encourage habit formation, but they are all variations of the three-step loop. When trying to develop a new habit, keep consistent and repeat as often as possible, plan ahead consciously, introduce cues and prompts, and break down bigger goals into smaller, more manageable milestones.
- When trying to break a bad habit, remember to address the physical, emotional, psychological, behavioral and environmental factors, too.
- When deciding on an appropriate technique for habit formation, first identify your overall goal, then outline the three steps of trigger, habit and reward, so you can make changes at each step.

Chapter 4. More of the Good, Less of the Bad

In previous examples, we've focused on pretty small and simple habits—things like eating better or being more active. The assumption, though, is that if we can incorporate these sorts of behaviors into our lives, we'll become healthier, happier people overall. The end goal is not to floss more or save a little extra money or stop swearing, but to develop our characters and evolve as human beings.

We are what we do. Whenever we strive to emulate a certain behavior, it's because on some level we want to be the kind of person associated with that behavior. So, the art of developing good habits is just the *how*; the *why* is to become better people, action by action, day by day. We do this not with blunt force, but intelligently: if the brain likes habits, well, give it habits. But make them good ones!

Commitment is better than willpower

You already "know" what you need to do. Work hard, live right, etc., etc. It's easy enough to see that we should change, but not so easy to actually do it. Yes, you can badly want to change, and you can thoroughly hate where you are right now. But still, this isn't enough to bring you from where you are to where you want to be. The missing element is not knowledge, or skill, or passion, or grit (although all these things are certainly useful). Rather, what's needed is commitment.

Commitment is what keeps you returning to your daily good habit, day after day, even when it's boring or difficult or painful. It's the easiest thing in the world to announce a resolution when all we have in our minds is the end result, and the satisfaction that comes with the achievement. But the end is just a small part of things—most of the journey is made of less exciting, smaller steps that are done daily and with diligence.

Again, though, this is not force or willpower, but simply the patience needed to commit—to choose a path and stay with it consistently. Habit can be thought of as the small units that build to create our big dreams. Commitment is the willingness to piece those dreams together, one step at a time. Passion and motivation may kick-start things but, just like in a marriage, commitment is needed to carry you through thick and thin, richer or poorer, as it were!

When we are feeling motivated, it's a good time to engage the goal-directed, conscious parts of our brain to make plans, appraise our current habits and actively rework our trigger-habit-reward loops. If we do this step correctly, and are patient as new habits take root, then we can eventually disengage the goal-directed brain and fall back on automatic behaviors to carry us.

With good habits, we can still work toward our goals and stay on track even on days we feel lazy and unable to spare much mental energy. When we have energy and motivation, we can build the systems and mechanisms to carry us automatically during those times we lack that energy. It's a matter of behavioral momentum.

Perhaps one of the biggest misconceptions in personal development is that one needs to be *inspired* to change, and that just because the end goal would feel amazing, the process should also feel amazing. Many of us unconsciously believe that being better should feel good, and that if the process feels uncomfortable, unfamiliar or difficult, it's proof we're doing something wrong—and so we quit before we've even started.

Picture someone wanting to lose a lot of weight. They may be fired up with enthusiasm and inspiration—the higher parts of their conscious brain see all the logical reasons to try and lose weight, and they look ahead to the end goal, and decide that it's what they want. To feel better. To look better. It's easy to say "yes!" to that vision.

But you already know how the story goes: after some of the initial fire and enthusiasm burns away, the parade of temptations and triggers comes along, and the person discovers just how powerful these urges are: they succumb to the old habit almost instantly. The grand goal seems so big and far away, whereas the cream bun in front of them is so close, so easy, and would feel good *right now*...

When you are committed, you don't expect things to be easy. You are prepared for any eventuality, because in a way it doesn't matter. Whatever the conditions, your work is always the same: do the habit as you planned, nothing more, nothing less. You are able to be consistent. You are able to make gradual improvements, a fraction of a percent at a time.

You barely register these little changes day to day, but over a year, say, the cumulative results are significant. You are not disappointed when you step on the scale and see only a pound has budged in weeks.

You are not comparing this small improvement to the monumental amount of weight you're ultimately hoping to shift, and so you can see each small gain for what it is: a step in the right direction.

At first, do the tiniest thing possible. Not possible? Then make it even tinier. Just keep moving forward. It's a great psychological trick for when you're feeling unmotivated—even if you're sick one day, you can still get up, do a *single* push-up, and go back to bed. In your mind, you've honored your commitment to keeping fit and have maintained an unbroken chain. Commitment is better than willpower; volume and intensity are less important than consistency.

Shortcuts and cheat codes would be nice, but life isn't like that. No matter how magnificent your ultimate goal, the path that leads to it inevitably contains some mundane and tedious parts. Let go of the idea of needing to be super-disciplined, extra-smart or badass—just get on with the hard work, today. Then tomorrow, do it again.

The irony is that these smaller goals get you to the end faster and more reliably. True, making tiny improvements here and there doesn't seem like much, but on the other hand, it's not too difficult or overwhelming. Who could be intimidated by having to tick off such a small step in the process?

A good rule of thumb is to focus on *process, not outcome*. Stay in the present with what can be done, right here and now. Focus on the habits you can build and maintain. Concentrate on the very next step, not the next forty steps. Decide on your big goal but then forget about it; keep your nose to the ground instead, where the real hard work is done.

Keep track of your progress, self-monitor and give yourself a reward for every step you take. Some days, simply turning up is enough. Some days, you can do a little more. Forgive missteps easily and move on. If you slip up, return to your good habit as soon as possible—there's no point in turning a small mistake into a bigger one because you feel bad about it.

Finally, don't do it alone. The American Society of Training and Development (ASTD) found in a study that by sharing your commitment with another person, you give yourself a 65 percent chance of completing it, which goes up to 95 percent if you schedule an "accountability appointment" to track and appraise your progress. So, externalize your commitment by making it public and letting others help keep you accountable.

Other people can serve as triggers for better behavior, or as rewards to reinforce the right habit when they offer praise, support and acknowledgment of your achievements. When you think about it, humans are social animals, and the habits we form are never developed in isolation. We don't need to change them in isolation, either. Share your plans and goals with those closest to you and you might be surprised at how willing they are to step in and do their part to help.

Establishing a new healthy habit is simple, but not easy. Decide on a goal, choose an action that helps get you closer to that goal, then plan when and how you'll complete that action. Make sure you're reinforcing the trigger-habit-reward loop and keep consistent. Be patient and committed for the sixty to ninety days it takes for the habit to stick. Simple.

There is a more fundamental skill being mastered in the background, however, as you engage in this process. By cultivating patience and discipline, by consciously setting goals that align with your values, and by deliberately working with your own unconscious mind, **you are developing the skill of all skills: the ability to learn, and change, and evolve.** This is a skill that will never lose value, and will enrich your life no matter how you choose to use it.

Developing a keystone habit and other good habits

It's in this spirit that we can start to talk about "keystone habits," or those good habits that seem to ripple out and inspire a host of other good habits. Earlier we discussed different kinds of habits— physical, intellectual or character ones. Out of these, which do you think has the greatest potential to make a real difference in your life?

Generally, the "higher" habits tend to be most powerful because they can influence lower habits, in a top-down way. For example, if you have a strong character habit of patience, you automatically improve your physical habits (like exercising and not becoming impatient with incremental gains in the gym) and intellectual habits (you are patient enough to push through and read a difficult book and learn something). Physical and intellectual habits can certainly lead to character habits in the long term (i.e. from the bottom up), but they don't necessarily do so. You probably know of a person who is in brilliant physical condition and is quite smart, but nevertheless doesn't have their life together!

A keystone habit is like the ultimate character habit, and it's great because it allows a degree of focus—pay attention to the single most important habit, and the rest naturally follow. For an example, it might be easier to start with *bad* keystone habits.

Take poor time management, for example, which may come down to a general attitude of avoidance and procrastination. It's not hard to see how everything in life could be impacted by this habit/attitude—you'd be late to romantic dates and job interviews, miss deadlines, and generally annoy everyone around you. What's more, any effort to improve on small unrelated habits would be negatively affected by your poor time management. For example, you might try to attend a weekly exercise class but consistently miss the first ten minutes.

A good keystone habit, on the other hand, could be something like daily meditation, a commitment to constantly reading and learning about new things, or good dietary habits that support a lifetime of health and vitality. As we've already seen, no two people will have the same keystone habits because we all have different challenges, values and goals. We all have different priorities based on our life stage, too—what seems most important to you as a young adult will definitely change as you get older, have children, or move through other life transitions.

Nevertheless, there are a few broad categories of keystone habits you might like to consider when thinking about the habits that will best serve you in your life.

Physical keystone habits

Good health is about as fundamental as it gets. Though good physical habits won't help you get into MENSA or solve your marriage problems, both these tasks will certainly be easier with physical health than without. If we hope to be successful in the physical domain, we inevitably need to focus on good diet and physical activity or exercise. If this is your keystone habit, so many other things fall into place: you may increase your longevity, avoid disease, improve your sex life, look better, have more energy, be more resilient, maintain a better mood and age more slowly.

Though some people seem to manage for a while, it's hard to imagine achieving higher goals when you eat garbage all day, drink, smoke and never exercise. Your brain, after all, is a part of your body, and if you don't take care of your body, it deteriorates and simply doesn't work as well. Your motivation, your passion, your cognitive ability—these are not possible to maintain if you are physically compromised.

Examples of physical keystone habits: a daily run, a consistent supplement regime, getting a comprehensive yearly checkup, stretching every day before bed, fasting, avoiding junk food, drinking plenty of water daily, having good sleep hygiene, avoiding alcohol.

Intellectual keystone habits

Isn't it interesting how many great people attribute their success to daily reading? Strengthening your critical faculties, thinking analytically, expanding your language abilities and learning new things are perhaps the most transferable skills that exist. When you have intellectual keystone habits, you become a master at learning itself, and every activity you engage in is improved. Intellectual habits include reading, writing, learning (skills and knowledge), teaching, or engaging in the arts or languages.

Examples of intellectual keystone habits: participating in a debate club, playing chess or other strategy games, reading textbooks and other manuals, taking online courses or short diplomas, learning to speak well in public, studying philosophy, learning a new language, studying formally at university or even regular travelling—one of the most mind-opening experiences out there!

Emotional keystone habits

Often neglected, these habits may actually do the most to equip a person to live a productive, meaningful life. Nobody is an island—we all relate to others, and we relate as emotional beings. At the root of many of our habits lie feelings, memories, fears, and desires. Learning to master the emotional aspect of our human experience means all our activities are enhanced. However, emotional habits can be tricky to pinpoint because you are the only one who can measure them, and they are often hard to distinguish from good character traits or emotional intelligence.

Examples of emotional keystone habits: routinely asking for feedback and help (and accepting it!), taking responsibility, attending therapy to work on yourself, being honest and speaking up for yourself, knowing how to consistently maintain good boundaries and having "emotional hygiene," working hard to be self-aware and humble, having self-compassion, and so on.

Spiritual keystone habits

Some people would confidently tell you that spiritual habits underpin everything else in their lives, be it via meditation, communing with nature, prayer, charity, creativity or contemplation. These are the habits that plug a person into a higher sense of purpose, and fuel them with the kind of energy that can only come from knowing they're part of a bigger whole. This might look like daily journaling to engage with your inner voice or intuition, doing community work to ground yourself, or regularly holding yourself accountable to your life's vision beyond the mundane.

Even if you don't consider yourself religious or find some of this a bit "out there," it's worth asking how you can support your own higher, spiritual dimensions, however you conceptualize of them. Many people find themselves forced to consider this aspect of life only after they've achieved an objectively successful life, yet still feel empty and lost. At the very least, a little self-reflection will help you tune in to the single habit that will best serve your life, right now.

Much of the self-help literature out there focuses on small, specific habits like drinking more water, stretching, smiling at strangers, sleeping well, reading, pausing for five minutes of mindfulness, avoiding saying "um" or "like" in conversations or having better posture. But if you pick just one or two keystone habits, all of these little habits fall into place.

For example, you could commit to daily journaling and meditation, which indirectly improves your self-esteem and self-awareness, which affects everything from the way you talk to people to your dietary choices to how you deal with adversity. By cultivating one big habit, you encourage dozens of smaller ones.

Ask yourself:

- In what areas of life do I currently experience the most challenge, or have the most room to grow?
- What kind of keystone habit would serve this need best?
- Make a list of various activities you could do toward this keystone habit. On the list, which is the *single* habit that will have the *greatest* effect?
- Focus on this habit. What is the smallest *sustainable* action you can take toward this habit, every day? For example, you could read just ten pages, walk fifteen minutes or cut down on one cigarette per day.

Breaking away from bad habits

As we've seen, the best way to "break" a bad habit is not to break it at all, but to replace it or transform it. Working with habits is always best done on two levels—i.e. acquiring good habits and losing bad ones. They need to be done together. If you quit smoking but find yourself fidgeting and craving something, you could end up picking up a new bad habit of overeating instead, thus defeating the purpose. The overall effort fails because you got rid of the bad, but didn't foster the good.

On the other hand, you could commit to eating more fruit and vegetables in a bid to be healthier, and actually achieve this goal. But it might not mean much when you look at your other habit of eating three donuts a day, undoing all your hard work to be healthier. The overall effort fails because you fostered the good but didn't do anything to get rid of the bad.

So, the smart strategy is to work simultaneously to reduce bad habits while building good ones—and what better way to do this than to literally convert your bad habits into better ones?

Identifying the bad habit

If you're one of those people who already knows what all their bad habits are, well, that's something to be proud of. But even still, are you *sure* you're 100 percent aware of all the routine behaviors that are currently holding you back? Even if it's not a bad habit per se, are you really doing things in the ideal way they could possibly be done?

Think about it: the hallmark of a habit is that it's automatic, and that you do it without thinking about it. This means that your most stubborn and harmful habits may actually be ones you've never even realized you had.

So how do you see something that your brain is not accustomed to even noticing?

Knowing what we know about routinized behavior, we can look for signs of automatic, unconscious habits, particularly ones that are harmful to us. We might not be conscious during the habit, but we can look for signs of it before and after. A big red flag is what's called cognitive dissonance—this refers to the mismatch between your actions and your purported beliefs and values.

For example, you love animals and care about animal welfare, and you believe eating meat is wrong, but you keep doing it. Or maybe you consider yourself a writer but somehow haven't put a single word to paper for years.

If you can identify such mismatches in your daily life, chances are there are some learnt, ingrained behaviors lurking underneath. It's not enough to simple know what the right thing is, or to intellectually grasp why the habit is bad for you. If you find yourself saying things like, "I know it's bad but I can't help doing X," then it's likely that X is habitual behavior—if it wasn't, your rational mind would be able to consciously choose to behave differently.

Watch to see if you make efforts to find the upside of behavior you know is bad for you, i.e. "Look, three donuts a day is excessive, I know, but I think of it as self-care—it's basically my Prozac!" This is called rationalization, and it's a defense mechanism designed to shield you from the uncomfortable fact that you're behaving directly against your own interests. You tell yourself, in a bizarre way, that acting against your best interests *is* in your best interests.

Watch for behaviors that you feel completely powerless to stop, even though you know you should, or try to. The automaticity of a behavior is a dead giveaway that it's been conditioned in you via the three-step loop—look closer and you can probably see the trigger and reward holding it in place. Notice if you ever feel like you're running on autopilot, completely checked out. Do you kind of "come to" after a behavior and feel as though you weren't even there, driving it? Well, "you" probably weren't—your basal ganglia just took over.

Try to notice when you feel compelled to act for seemingly no reason—you might have just been triggered without knowing it. Just because your unconscious mind is following well-entrenched cues, it doesn't mean your conscious mind knows anything about it. Fast-food advertisers bank on this response—if you've ever had a sudden mad craving for McDonalds', look back and ask if you inadvertently triggered a craving by seeing someone eat a Big Mac on a TV ad, for example.

Recall, also, that behavior and cognition don't operate in a vacuum; emotion is a big part of the equation, too. Certain emotional clues can indicate the presence of habitual behavior. Look for sudden shifts in mood, or watch how certain behaviors alter how you feel. Are you reaching for something to calm you down or pep you up? Is a certain habit serving as a distraction or coping mechanism?

Finally, an obvious way to spot an unconscious habit that is truly bad for you is to look for the results of it in your life, for example in your relationships or work life. Are certain behaviors threatening or undermining your ability to connect with others, to earn a living, to be a good parent, to stay healthy, and so on?

Destructive bad habits aren't just big things like drug addictions; they include annoying habits that alienate people, or work habits that get you in trouble or compromise your performance in serious ways. If people *consistently* complain about how you interrupt, or show up late to everything, or put the photocopier on the wrong setting, then it's probably time to pay attention!

Finally, though we're talking about obvious behaviors like substance misuse or addictions, some of our most self-defeating habits are all about what we *don't* do. Turning down social invites, avoiding medical checkups, procrastinating on exercise...these are not so much bad behaviors as the absence of good ones.

In trying to identify bad habits in your life, don't only look for obvious harm or damage. Look also at all the ways you shortchange yourself by not going further, not pushing harder, or not taking risks. You might find that you have a more abstract, harder to notice habit of being too risk averse, or withdrawing socially when stressed. These tendencies are harder to spot, but impact your life negatively all the same.

Breaking the bad habit

It all starts with being mindful of one's actions. Being aware of ourselves and our behavior is half the battle won. Habits are *unconscious*. We begin to gain control of them when we make them *conscious*, and choose to move ahead with deliberate intention instead. In other words, we stop being backseat passengers in our lives and start to be the drivers of our own behavior.

One great "keystone habit" is to simply force yourself as often as possible to come into consciousness, and understand *why* you are performing certain behaviors. You don't need to do formal sitting meditation, just refuse to take anything at face value. Why are you having another drink/ignoring your friend's call/buying that gadget? How do feel right now, after behaving that way, and what does that mean? Why did you just do what you did? What was the result?

Step out of the shortcut and come out of autopilot. Watch what your brain does, rather than just being at the mercy of what it does. With this simple shift in perspective, you are empowered to be a conscious agent rather than a slave to your ingrained conditioning.

It may seem simple, but this is the first and nonnegotiable step to loosening the hold of a bad habit. Once you are aware of what you're doing, you can manipulate the triggers/cues as well as the rewards to elicit the behaviors you want. The principles below come from the classical behaviorist perspective in psychology, i.e. by understanding the mechanisms of behavior, cause and effect, pleasure and pain, you can predict or even control that behavior.

- Use **positive reinforcement** to stimulate dopamine release and direct it to a target of your choosing. Positive reinforcement is adding something pleasurable. A bad habit stimulates dopamine release, too, so you'll need to create a reward that rivals it. How can you make it pleasurable and rewarding to *not* perform the old habit? You could try to quit smoking by making it so that every dollar you don't spend on cigarettes gets spent toward something you like even more. On the other hand, you could replace smoking with another habit that feels as good or better, like chewing gum. Use positive reinforcement to destroy a trigger, for example removing tempting snacks from the kitchen.

- Use **negative reinforcement**, i.e. taking something away to increase the chances of a behavior occurring. When the alarm in your car pings loudly until you put your seat belt on, it's using negative reinforcement to shape your behavior. The reward is, in effect, the removal of something irritating. Nagging guilt or constant reminders are ways to ensure you do the behavior you're trying to make habitual. One way to accomplish this is with, well, guilt. If other people hold you accountable, you may act just to avoid disappointing them or embarrassing yourself. Naturally, negative reinforcement works better to create good habits than to eliminate bad ones.

- Use **punishment** to decrease pleasure or add pain/discomfort to make a behavior less likely. Doing the bad habit stimulates dopamine release and reinforces positive feelings, but you can undermine this effect by associating the habit with the removal of pleasure, too. So, with every cigarette you smoke, your friend is allowed to take ten dollars from your bank account to give to charity. Make your habit boring, humiliating, unpleasant or difficult to do. Some people freeze their credit cards in giant blocks of ice, so they need to wait for them to thaw before they can use them to make impulse purchases. Using bitter nail varnish to stop nail biting is also a punishment—what used to cause pleasure now only elicits disgust.

Working with pleasure/punishment and manipulating the triggers/rewards can give you control over automatic habits. As long as you remember that your brain is constantly finding shortcuts and making associations, you can ensure it's making ones that favor the habits you're trying to develop. By bringing mindfulness to your thoughts, feelings and actions, you can zoom in on the pleasure and reward you derive, and rework it.

When you are aware, change is possible. As you eat the unhealthy food or procrastinate or take a harmful substance, you are *aware* of what it does to your body, your mind, your relationships, your well-being. You are *aware* that it's not logically a good choice. Make it harder on yourself to perform actions that are incompatible with your values; increase cognitive dissonance until it becomes so obvious and uncomfortable you can't ignore it anymore.

Though conscious awareness is not enough on its own (we've seen that unconscious conditioned responses can be stronger), it can help to educate yourself on what your habit really costs you. Reframe your action in a way that downplays its positives and emphasizes its negatives.

Let's say you're someone who can't seem to curb an online shopping addiction. By becoming more aware, you notice other behaviors keeping this habit in place—the fact that you never check bank statements, that you always come up with excuses and justifications to spend, that you promptly forget about what you've bought after the thrill of purchasing it is gone.

A spending addiction can be serious, but you might approach the problem by thinking of your other values. By educating yourself, you bring home the real cost of your habit: you indirectly fund exploitative industries and overseas sweatshops to get those deals, you fritter away money you could spend on your children's future, savings, or a million other better things, you gather data about just how much has been spent so far...

Straightforward punishment and reward are one thing, but there's a lot to be said for expanding your conscious awareness of what your behavior really involves, and what it's doing to you and others. Using positive and negative reinforcement can also help interrupt automatic bad habits, but they're best thought of as short-term solutions. In the longer term, this shift in perspective helps you become aware of how that habit is functioning in your life, and can help you release it voluntarily.

Better yet, don't break them, replace them

Let's take a closer look at practical ways to bring together what we've learnt, so that we're simultaneously reducing bad habits while building up good ones. We keep the trigger and keep the reward, but we switch out the middle part—the habit itself.

For example, instead of drinking alcohol when out socializing, you switch to a non-alcoholic replacement. You are still triggered by your friends inviting you out, and by going to a bar, and you still get the reward of having something to hold and swirl around as you socialize, but you have removed the harmful alcohol habit and replaced it with something harmless.

If you're mindful and paying attention, you can dig deep to understand the emotional aspect of your habits, which will tell you where the reward lies. Then, you can find a convincing substitute. If you become aware that you are consistently triggered to waste time online and on social media because of boredom or exhaustion, notice when boredom appears and commit to doing something else that's interesting and beneficial instead, or else take it as a sign you need a nap.

Break out of habits by inviting the new and the fresh—change up your environment, or change the people you hang around with. Take a different route to work or do the opposite of what you ordinarily do, just to see what happens. Doing all this can kick your brain out of autopilot and get you more conscious and asking, is there something *better* I could be doing right now?

Chances are, you may discover that the rewards keeping your old habits in place aren't even all that great. Maybe they brought you pleasure at one time in your life, or they feel good relative to something else, but when you look closely, it's not enough of a benefit to keep you repeating the same harmful behaviors.

Instead, your *perception* of the benefit is what keeps you trapped. And perceptions can change. When you are mindful of what you're really doing in the moment, you can look at these habits more honestly and make updates. Is spending hours and hours on social media really all that satisfying after all?

Turn the trigger-habit-reward loop on its head and use what have been called the "3 Rs": reminder, routine and reward. Your triggers could be a certain time of day, a place, the presence of certain people, your emotional state, or a particular action you always follow up with another particular action. Use any of these to your advantage and reframe them as reminders to do something else, something better.

One way to do this methodically is to identify the bad habit you want to replace and gather as much data about it as possible. Write down the time, place, preceding actions and overall emotional state that accompanies this habit. For example, if the bad habit you want to break is wasting hours on your phone:

Place: on the bus to work

Time: 9 a.m.

Emotional state: bored and stressed

Preceding action/trigger: getting ready for work, boarding the bus

Reward: distraction, boredom relief

Effect of the habit: stressed out further

Do the above for as many different discreet moments as you notice yourself doing the behavior. This may take a few days, but be patient. Your goal is to look for patterns. Before you start to make changes, you need to arm yourself with information, and beyond this, you need to feel confident and able to make realistic changes. It's almost always better to start small and take baby steps.

Look at the notes you've gathered and ask what you have the ability to change. For the above entry, consider *why* you're reaching for your phone to perform your bad habit— you're bored and stressed, and to be honest, there's nothing else to do on the bus anyway. Maybe you notice a lot of entries like this—whenever you reach for your phone, it's because you're at a loose end and don't know what to do with yourself.

You also notice, however, that scrolling through stressful news stories or forums actually makes you feel worse. It might not be until you literally put it down on paper that you see how nonsensical it all is: the thing you do because you're stressed ends up stressing you more. So, you don't get much from the behavior at all.

Noticing these patterns, you make a plan. What behavior can you adopt that actually will help you reduce stress and alleviate boredom, but in a healthier way? You decide you're going to experiment with reading instead. You pick a few books you've been meaning to read for a while (but "never had the time") and, thinking ahead, you place one in the pouch in your bag where you normally keep your phone.

Now, when it's nine a.m. and you feel bored and stressed, and you reach for your phone, you don't find your phone but a book instead. You read it. Maybe you wish you could scroll through your phone instead, but you stick with the replacement. You only read those books that you genuinely like, and take a moment to tell yourself, "I love reading." Within a few weeks, you can track your progress: your screen time is down and you feel less stressed in the mornings. Success!

Now, it might not work immediately. You may have to pay attention and make adjustments as you go. Maybe after a while you realize that reading isn't a good replacement, because it wasn't the words on your screen you were conditioned to do, but more the fidgeting and fiddling behavior of scrolling itself. So, you make a plan and reach for a fidget toy or even bring some knitting with you, so you have something semi-mindless but relaxing to do as you travel to work.

All of this might seem painfully obvious, but that's kind of the point—to make what seemed automatic and unconscious more conscious. Most people are very surprised at some of the things they find out about themselves when they open their mind and *really look* at their behaviors, their triggers, their rewards.

Adopt the perspective of a neutral scientist simply observing and finding patterns. Take nothing as a given. What is it exactly that is so attractive about a particular habit? Most of the time, the reward you seek by doing a habit is something natural and human—which means there's a healthy, "normal" way to satisfy that need directly.

We all want to feel good in life, to feel as though people care about us, to have a life that means something, to experience novelty and excitement, and to feel confident and safe in who we are. If you can find smart and healthy ways to satisfy these perfectly natural needs, you release yourself from the grip of bad habits, and in time may even start to wander why you ever thought you needed them!

Takeaways:

- Habits are mental heuristics designed to save mental energy, time and effort—you don't need sheer force or willpower to develop good habits, only an understanding of how they naturally develop, plus enough commitment and discipline to stick to the plan you choose for yourself.

- It's OK to make mistakes, to be lazy or feel unmotivated, but with good habits what matters is staying consistent, no matter what.
- Small incremental changes that add up are the key to reaching big goals; our focus should be on process and not outcome.
- Making yourself accountable to others by sharing your commitment makes it more likely that you will maintain your habit and achieve your goal.
- A keystone habit is a meta-habit that inspires many smaller, related habits. By focusing on the development of the keystone habit that matters most to you, you don't need to work to build dozens of smaller habits.
- Keystone habits can be physical, intellectual, emotional or spiritual, and they ultimately encourage the cultivation of a stronger, happier and more resilient character.

- Breaking bad habits is difficult but not impossible. Since many of us are oblivious to the existence of our bad habits, we need honesty and self-awareness to become conscious of why we're really behaving as we are.
- To identify a bad habit, look for defense mechanisms like over-rationalizing, cognitive dissonance, emotional irregularity, automatic behavior you can't seem to control, and negative effects to your health, relationships or work life.
- You can use positive reinforcement, negative reinforcement or punishment to move yourself away from a bad habit, i.e. increasing the pain or decreasing the pleasure associated with the habit, or else increasing the pleasure associated with an alternative habit. Manipulating triggers and rewards allows you to decrease the likelihood of the behavior recurring.
- It's easier to replace a habit than to eliminate it. Keep the trigger and

reward the same but replace the habit itself with a more positive one.

Chapter 5. How to Short Circuit Yourself

By now, it should be clear that when it comes to working effectively with habits, you need a comprehensive approach that starts from the fundamentals. Having covered those fundamentals, we can now take a look at some of the most common behavioral modification techniques out there. But now, you should be able to see clearly *why* they can be so effective, what to avoid, and how to tailor each approach so that it best fits your unique situation.

Some of the following methods we've hinted at already, and some won't be unfamiliar to you. However, before picking a technique and trying to apply it to your life, remind yourself to keep the basic three-step loop at the back of your mind. Remember what a habit is (automatic, unconscious, repeated) so you know exactly how to work around it. Most of all, **remember that nothing that works will work instantly**—even the most effective approach will still take commitment, patience and mindful repetition. Let's jump in.

Control your impulses

One great way to master positive habit formation is to learn to control your impulses. They are polar opposites; one is stable and reliable like a metronome, while the other is unpredictable like a volcano.

An impulse is the sudden need to do (or not do) something, an uncontrollable urge. Impulses are often acted upon without forethought or planning and can come out of nowhere to derail your entire day. This is where habit dies, because you are at the mercy of a spur-of-the-moment whim. You can't engage in both at the same time.

Control over impulses is a key to consistent discipline.

For instance, imagine that you are playing piano during a big performance, but you get the sudden impulse to scratch an itch on your face. The itch is not urgent, nor is it important, but it's something nagging in the back of your mind that will cause you discomfort unless you address it. Now, will you break your performance to scratch the itch, or will you ignore the temporary distraction? You would probably recognize that your impulse should take a back seat to maintaining habit in this instance.

Only rarely, like in the above example, is it clear that we should suppress these random impulses. But just like the piano performance, we don't realize how much indulging in an impulse will throw us off. These things add up, and so does the time required for you to re-focus yourself and get back on the horse of habit.

How can we defeat this type of enemy? First, we must understand it.

Impulses have been the subject of psychological research for many years. Recently, researchers from the European Molecular Biology Laboratory have found strong connections between two parts of the brain related to impulse control: the prefrontal cortex, the part of the brain responsible for complex cognition, personality, decision-making, and social behavior; and the brainstem, the portion of the brain that regulates basic autonomic functions such as heart rate and breathing.

This means we possess a significant number of connections that allow us to self-regulate and control ourselves—it takes a conscious thought in our prefrontal cortex, and it travels to our brainstem for calm and relaxation. When we have a strong link between the two, we can better exercise habits.

However, in the study, scientists found that a condition known as *social defeat* (a negative emotional state) in mice weakened the connection between the prefrontal cortex and the part of the brainstem involved in defensive responses. With a weaker connection, the mice became more impulsive, wilder, and difficult to calm down. When the researchers used a drug to block the connection between the prefrontal cortex and the brainstem completely, the mice demonstrated even more impulsive behavior.

How does this translate to humans? This research sheds light on what is happening in your brain when you're trying to control an impulse. If we're in an emotional state, the connection between the prefrontal cortex and the brainstem is weakened. We become more impulsive and less self-aware.

We can't very well take drugs to strengthen our neural connections and maintain habits, but we can try to ensure that our prefrontal cortex is engaged as much as possible. That roughly translates to making decisions based on analysis and rationality versus emotion. Habit won't win in the face of urgency, anxiety, and fear, so you have to let those feelings pass and then keep on keeping on. When we're thinking with our brainstem, which isn't always something we can control, our habit goes out the window.

There are techniques we can implement to support our desire to better control our impulses. Generally, they involve some sort of delay between feeling the impulse and the reaction you give to it. In other words, the more distance between feeling the itch and scratching the itch, the better. You'll usually find that the impulse simply disappears on its own, which further proves its status as something that is simply masquerading as important (when it's really not).

The power of ten. If you can delay action on your impulses, often you can overcome them. There is something to be said for taking a breath, counting slowly to ten, and giving yourself a moment. Tell yourself to persevere for just ten more seconds when you want to stop, and tell yourself to try something out for just ten seconds when you are delaying starting. That's the power of ten—the mere act of holding yourself back requires habit, and you practice feeling a reaction without acting on it.

The power of ten takes the urgency out of your impulse to act immediately.

Remember, that's where your brainstem loses its grip over your actions and your prefrontal cortex steps in.

For some impulses, counting to ten won't suffice. For example, if you see something you want to buy but don't really *need*, instead of just taking it to the register to be rung up, you can wait ten minutes, the second power of ten. This is the same type of diversionary tactic that neuroscientists have found extremely effective to battle impulse-spending and shopping; just ten minutes drastically reduces the brain's thirsty response for a reward. Rather than rush to purchase the item, you could leave the store for ten minutes, and you'll be less likely to follow through with the purchase.

Usually, an itch will disappear within seconds. A strong emotional spike will mostly dissipate within ten seconds. You might stop seeing red in that time span. Your initial reaction just might have given way to rational thought.

After all, anyone can withstand anything for ten seconds, right? Keep this mantra in mind and bypass the danger zone where your brainstem is in control of your actions.

Label your feelings. A person who doesn't understand his or her emotions is more likely to act on impulse. If you can't identify when you're feeling angry or stressed or embarrassed, you may act in a way that just makes it worse. In essence, if you don't realize what you're feeling, you will be unable to stop it.

For example, suppose you have an argument with someone and you impulsively stomp off and slam the door on your way out. Those behaviors scream anger, but they likely happened so quickly, so impulsively, that you didn't consciously think—you just reacted.

If you took a moment to realize why you want to storm out the door and how angry you are, you would have a better chance of tempering your response. Instead of leaving in a huff, say, "I think I'm feeling angry right now. I should deal with the anger first and then respond after it passes." That takes the acute impulse out of the situation and increases the chance that things will go better once the situation is de-escalated. It also gives you an exact symptom—anger, resentment, bitterness, frustration—and from that you can find a roadmap to deal with it. That wouldn't be possible without a label.

It's acceptable to feel angry, embarrassed, frustrated, and ashamed. But what *isn't* acceptable is to substitute these initial reactions as your response and act impulsively. When you take a pause to identify what you're feeling, often you will realize that things aren't quite as urgent as you thought.

Write down the facts. Writing down the facts of a situation helps you clarify what is real, what is not, and what your ideal outcome is. This is related to the power of ten in that you are pausing to sort through the facts before you act impulsively with the brainstem. And of course, you write much more slowly than you think, so this slows your entire reactive process down. That bodes well for the prefrontal cortex and habit.

Thus, when you want to quit something, when you want to delay starting something, or when you suddenly feel an urge to do something unproductive or distracting, write down the facts. Write out what the situation is, what you want to do, and what you should probably do instead. Write down your ideal outcome and how that differs from the path you would take if you gave in to your impulse.

Highlight only what is factual and leave out the rest. Don't write down your feelings, emotions, fears, or anxieties. Keep it black and white. When you have a clear picture of "just the facts, ma'am," you are able to look at the situation objectively and know what you should do. This not only allows you to respond in a more tempered fashion, but it helps you sort out what actually happened versus what you "thought" or "felt" occurred.

For example, suppose you had a blow-up with your boss at work, and your impulse is to quit your job and look for a new one. Writing down the facts will help you clarify the situation and sort the emotion from the facts. Maybe the facts are your boss blamed you for a situation; you didn't get to tell your side of the story; you've worked at your current job for eight years; you are the primary breadwinner of your family; in addition to your salary, you have good benefits; and you haven't talked to human resources to help resolve the situation. You want to punch his face and quit—that doesn't get you to your ideal outcome. Your ideal outcome involves being heard, being more assertive, and keeping your job.

Suddenly, after taking the time to examine the facts, it's clear what you need to do to maintain habit. An impulse only exists because it is quick and fleeting; under greater scrutiny, they almost all crumble.

Ask "why" five times. A final strategy for helping to control your impulses is asking *why*. This tactic is all about getting to the root of your impulse and hopefully uncovering new information about yourself. You're actually asking the same or a similar question five times in a row, and you'll be surprised to learn that each time, you just might pull out a different answer than before. You're forcing yourself to justify why an impulse should win out over habit. At the end of the process, you'll either be able to answer *why* sufficiently, or you'll come to the conclusion that it was simply an impulse not worth partaking in.

Impulses are never thought through or founded on deep analysis, so you wouldn't expect to be able to answer *why* more than once or twice. Thus, only if you can answer *why* a few times does the matter pass the sniff test of importance or urgency. Practically speaking, what does this look like? Suppose you have an impulse to break your spending discipline and buy a new sweater.

Why do you want it?

I like it.

Why do you want it?

It's a great price. (This is as far as an impulse will probably carry you.)

Why do you want it?

No real reason other than wanting it...

Why do you want it?

Looks cool?

Why do you want it?

I guess I don't, really.

Once you've asked yourself *why* five times, in five different ways, you have distilled the main pros and cons for why you should or shouldn't buy the shirt. And really, you've come up with nothing to justify the impulse. If this was really a shirt that you needed in some way, you'd be able to come up with better answers, such as "Because my other shirt ripped" or "I have a wedding coming up" or "I want to look nice for a date!" In those instances, you are *not* dealing with an impulse masquerading as a need—it's an actual need.

Even if this technique doesn't bring you to the point where you realize you can't answer *why* five times (which is a red flag), at least it will force you to stop and think about your decisions. Whatever the outcome, you've become more mindful and more likely to be disciplined in your daily life.

Visualization: seeing is believing

In an earlier chapter, we spoke about using self-talk and visualization to trick the brain into believing something was already a habit. By drawing attention to or emphasizing the benefits of a good habit while ignoring the positives of a bad habit, you subtly make associations that cue your brain to want to repeat good habits instead of bad ones. Let's take a closer look at the technique of visualization, a simple but extremely effective tool in the quest for better habits.

Visualization happens before you lift a finger and is something that you can repeat ad nauseam to build a stronger *yes* response.

Visualization, quite simply put, is *detailed imagination*. You use your mind's eye to picture yourself executing whatever it is you're planning to accomplish. Visualization helps you build a sense of awareness and expectation. It's a mental rehearsal to understand the experience and associated emotions.

And believe it or not, it works. Australian researcher Alan Richardson ran a trial on visualization on a group of basketball players. He divided them into three different groups and gave each a twenty-day assignment involving free throws.

All of the groups physically practiced making free throws on the first and last days of the twenty-day period. One group was instructed to practice making free throws for twenty minutes every day. A second group was instructed to do nothing in between the first and twentieth days.

Finally, a third group was told only to "visualize" themselves making free throws between the first and last days of the trials. This process didn't just mean the players pictured themselves sinking shots successfully—it also included visualizing their *missing* free throws and *practicing* correcting their shot.

The results were eye-opening. The group that physically practiced for twenty days boosted their free throw success rate by 24 percent. But astonishingly, the visualization group also improved by 23 percent—almost as much as the practice squad. Not surprisingly, the group that did neither didn't improve at all.

The conclusion from this study is that visualization causes changes even when unaccompanied by actual physical work. The brain and its neural pathways can be conditioned and strengthened, just as muscles and the cardiovascular system can. Visualization can help align the brain with the physical execution of anything we do and can be a great means of additional support in our efforts. Seeing is believing, no matter the type of seeing.

Use this tool to make yourself, well, whatever you want to be. For instance, visualize a situation you are afraid of and make all the tough, disciplined, and unpleasant choices in your mind. Play it through with as many details as possible. How does it feel? We can start to understand that our fear is rooted in ignorance, and we can start to build a relationship with the feeling of comfort in discomfort. Almost all of us hesitate and want to retreat to a comfort zone when confronted with something foreign. Make risky situations as familiar as possible by visualizing them and this instinct will decrease accordingly.

Visualization is easy, but as with any process, it works best with guided steps. It is helpful to approach visualization as meditation—a quiet but concentrated immersion into your thoughts and imagination. One particularly effective technique involves five steps.

1. Relaxation. The first step involves getting yourself into a tranquil state, physically and mentally. It includes techniques like finding a quiet spot, taking deep and measured breaths, and closing your eyes to enter a meditative state.

2. Imagining the environment. The second step is building a detailed mental picture of the situation, surroundings, and specific objects you'll be working with when you finally take action.

3. Viewing the scene as a third person. The third part of this method is picturing yourself doing an activity the way someone else would—how you'd appear in the eyes of someone watching you.

4. Viewing as first person. The fourth part is an intensive imagining of yourself doing the activity—how your senses and emotions would react and feel while you're doing it.

5. Coming back to reality. The final part involves *slowly* reemerging from your visualization into the physical world, ready to take on the challenge for real.

Let's try a sample visualization with a situation that can cause some to feel utter panic and terror: delivering a speech. It doesn't seem as challenging as jumping out of an airplane or taking part in a sword fight, but some of the toughest people in the world have trepidation about standing in front of a polite audience and speaking directly to them. Build your *yes* response and quiet your *no* response. Applying the above five steps, here's how that visualization might go.

1. Relax. Find a quiet spot where you won't be disturbed or interrupted for a few minutes—lying on a couch or bed with the windows and doors closed. Breathe deeply from your stomach. Take as much time as you need to let all areas of tension in your body dissipate. Finally, close your eyes.

2. Imagine the environment. Make a detailed survey of the room and space where you'll be making your speech. Picture the chairs the audience will sit in. Imagine the lighting and feel of the room, from how bright the overhead lamps might be to the air-conditioning. Is the stage raised above the floor? Is there a podium you'll be standing behind? Will there be a microphone, or will you be wearing a headset? Imagine how either looks, down to the foam piece over the microphone head or the tiny earphones.

3. View the scene as a third person. Now you're somebody in the audience watching as you speak. You see yourself dressed in a suit, standing upright, delivering words clearly and directly, raising your pitch to make a point or lowering your voice to make a joke. You're seeing all the hand gestures, head tilts, and facial expressions you'd see if you were watching the speech instead of giving it.

4. View as first person. At this point you go back into yourself, giving the speech and addressing the audience. You can hear how your words sound in your head. You note the distance from your mouth to the microphone. You can see the audience members' faces as they're paying attention. You hear the reverb from your voice echoing throughout the room, whether it's a little or a lot. You feel your hands resting on the wood surface of the podium. You see the words printed on the page you're reading from—or you see yourself moving around the stage without a script. You sense how your body's reacting: the nervous energy in your gut, the clarity in your head, the blood flow in your arms and legs. You hear the applause at the end, down to each individual handclap.

5. Wrap it up. You let the scene fade to black (or white if you prefer) in your head. You spend a few moments slowly coming back to the present, remembering the scene that's just transpired and marking each feeling you'll look out for when you're giving the speech. Recall specifically all the choices you made that were bold and daring as opposed to conservative and fearful. Then you gently open your eyes.

Somehow that visualization has made speech-giving seem terribly exciting. Imagine what it can do for parachuting and sword fighting.

We call the previously described process "visualization," but that phrasing isn't entirely accurate, since most people associate visualization with seeing things with one's eyes. A more exact term for this process might be *multi-sensory imagination* or *mental rehearsal,* because the full process draws from all of the senses we possess:

Visual: sense of sight

Auditory: sense of hearing

Kinesthetic: sense of touch

Olfactory: sense of smell

Gustatory: sense of taste

It might be easiest for us to imagine visuals during mental rehearsal, but never underestimate the power of the other four senses, as well as emotional sensations. They're responsible for some of our strongest memories: the sound of a band, the smell of a rainy afternoon, the taste of an ice cream sundae, or the touch of a fuzzy sweater. During visualization, try as hard as you can to incorporate those other senses as well as how your scene looks to the eye.

Studies have shown that our brain chemistry treats imagined memories— visualization, that is—the same way as it treats *actual* memories. If you can visualize to a deep level, using all five senses and emotional projections, your brain is going to instill the scene as something you've already experienced. When you visualize jet-skiing, playing professional football, or being shot out of a cannon, your brain is just going to assume you've actually done so. You might logically know better, but emotionally you will be more even-keeled and calm, ready to tackle adversity.

This can be key in building your *yes* response. When you're about to do something you've never done before, most of the anxiety and tension you feel happens *before* you actually start doing it. The nervousness you experience in a new endeavor usually comes up when you're anticipating doing it. When you're actually doing it, most of that anxiety goes away.

Therefore, if the brain treats visualization the same way it treats real memories, you can trick your brain into building a belief in yourself. Sure, you might only be *visualizing* sky-diving, but if you do it thoroughly enough, your brain is going to understand that the fear that leads to a *no* response isn't necessary or even helpful.

The If/then technique
Even if you aren't, your brain is already very familiar with conditionals, i.e. if/then statements. After all, this is exactly what the three-step behavior loop is: the brain remembers that the last time a trigger occurred, and it performed the related behavior, a pleasurable reward followed. In other words, "If I do this behavior in a

certain environment when a certain trigger occurs, then I can expect the same outcome."

A helpful technique that directly deals with the relationship between the cue and the routine as described in Duhigg's habit loop is the if-then technique. This is also sometimes known as an *implementation intention*—in other words, making your intention easy to implement. The *if* portion corresponds to the cue, while the *then* portion refers to the routine.

The simple fact is that there's a big gap between knowing what you want to do and actually getting it done. Whatever the obstacles—distractions, inefficiencies, or procrastination—wearing neural grooves through consistent action will make the habit easier.

If-then statements take the following form: if X happens, then I will do Y. That's it. This is something you decide in advance, and there are two primary ways to use it. This makes it easier to build habits because all you have to do is plug your desired action in as a natural consequence of something that is certain to happen. When actions are chained and given forethought, they tend to actually occur.

As a quick example, *if* it is 3:00 p.m. on Sunday, *then* you will call your mother. Or more specific to habits you might want to cultivate, *if* it is 3:00 p.m., *then* you will drink two liters of water, or if it is 9:00 p.m., then you will floss your teeth. These are examples of when you use if-then to accomplish a specific goal, the first type of use. X can be whatever event, time, or occurrence you choose that happens on a daily basis, and Y is the specific action that you will take.

The if-then statement simply takes your goals and desired habits out of the ether and ties them to concrete moments in your day. A habit to eat healthier and drink more water has a set prescription, for instance, or a vow to maintain better dental health is carried out every day because it is contingent upon a daily occurrence. Instead of generalities, you get a time and place for when to act.

It seems simplistic, and it is, but it has been shown that you are two to three times more likely to succeed if you use an if-then plan than if you don't. In one study, 91 percent of people who used an if-then plan stuck to an exercise program versus 39 percent of non-planners. Peter Gollwitzer, the NYU psychologist who first articulated the power of if-then planning, recently reviewed results from ninety-four studies that used the technique and found significantly higher success rates for just about every goal you can think of, from using public transportation more frequently to avoiding stereotypical and prejudicial thoughts.

As you can imagine, this perceived lack of choice makes it easier to create the neuroplasticity you want—because there are no other paths. In a sense, it is like constructing an enriched environment for your mind because it leaves you with only one outcome, and thus the neural connections are forced to grow.

The primary reason if-then statements work so well is because they speak the language of your brain, which is the language of contingencies. Humans are good at encoding information in "If X, then Y" terms and using this process (often unconsciously) to guide our behavior. It's the basis of decision-making, which is often subconscious and instantaneous. The brain works by evaluating pros and cons, and it often happens in the limbic system without our recognition. That's the type of process we are intentionally creating.

Deciding exactly when and where you will act on your goal creates a link in your brain between the situation or cue (the *if*) and the behavior that should follow (the *then*).

Let's say your significant other has been giving you a hard time about forgetting to text to inform them that you will be working late and not make dinner. So you make an if-then plan: if it is 6:00 p.m. and I'm at work, then I will text my significant other. Now the situation "6:00 p.m. at work" is wired in your brain directly to the action "text my sugar bear."

Then the situation or cue "6:00 p.m. at work" becomes highly activated. Below your awareness, your brain starts scanning the environment, searching for the situation in the "if" part of your plan. Once the "if" part of your plan happens, the "then" part follows *automatically*. You don't *have* to consciously monitor your goal, which means your plans get carried out even when you are preoccupied.

The best part is that by detecting situations and directing behavior without conscious effort, if-then plans are far less taxing and require less willpower than mere resolutions. They enable us to conserve our habit for when it's really needed and compensate for it when we don't have enough mental energy. Armed with if-thens, you can tell your fickle friend willpower that this year, you really won't be needing him.

The second use of the if-then technique is also related to achieving a specific goal, but rather it helps us to avoid *failing* at that goal. You would still use if X then Y, but X would be an unexpected situation that you want to maintain control in and deal with. In the first use, X is simply any everyday situation, occurrence, or event. Here, X is something that may not happen but you want to be prepared for. For instance, if you want to create a habit of drinking water, *if* you eat out at a restaurant, *then* you will get water with lemon only. That's a situation that isn't certain to occur, but it helps you adhere to your habit from the opposite end.

Complete these statements *before* you are in a dire situation, and you can see how they work for you. It is like creating a rule for yourself to abide by. If you've given it thought beforehand, you can default to that guideline and not have to try to make a risky decision in the heat of the moment. Anticipate what's to happen and you are a step ahead of the game.

As another example, suppose it's your birthday, but you're on a strict diet and your office has a thing for surprise parties so you'll probably be getting one. "If they brought cake, then I'll turn it down and immediately drink a big glass of water." Alternatively, you could be having a problem with procrastination, and you're settling in for a big project you have to finish. You could say, "If the phone rings, then I'll ignore it until I'm done."

You can get more detailed with these statements and can prepare them for situations with more significance or danger than the above examples. But whatever the case, the if-then method forces you to project yourself into common scenarios that could trigger reversion to your bad habits— and makes you plan for those triggers. It takes away your residuals of false justification and excuses for doing the wrong thing (or doing nothing) and sharpens your commitment to meeting your goals.

All of these methods help focus on the minute but powerful triggers that lead us into the personal infractions we're trying to eliminate, and they help us overcome the resistance that arises from forcing change in our lives. Best of all, they don't rely on sweeping or exhaustive changes to who we are—they make our brains and natural impulses work *for* us instead of going to sleep on the job.

Once again, deciding exactly how you'll react to circumstances regarding your goal creates a link in your brain between the situation or cue (if) and the behavior that should follow (then.) And as we know, everything good that we want to happen begins in our brain.

Social and physical environment

Habits are ingrained because of our initial experiences with *triggers*—very few behaviors form spontaneously, in a vacuum. So if behaviors and habits are a result of conditioning from the environment, why is it that so much advice completely ignores the environment, and focuses on the isolated individual? Though each of us has a certain scope of agency and we all are responsible for our actions, our surroundings and the people we associate with make a big difference to the way we behave.

The biggest obstacle we face in changing our behaviors could very well be one we might think we have no way to control: our environment. It's a factor that's often overlooked or understated, but it can be the most potent source of support or the most lethal force of damage.

An environment can be the deciding element of whether something is possible, hopeless, or unavoidable. If you wanted to become a great piano player, how might your environment factor into your improvement or lack thereof? For instance, what if you lived in a piano warehouse? What if you didn't have access to a piano within driving distance? These are ways your environment can simply make something possible or impossible.

Supportive environments reinforce positive behaviors and cater to those who adhere to good practices. But unhelpful environments can produce fatigue and despondency in people who must fight to flourish. An inferior environment is often the real cause of problems that some might attribute to failures of will, discipline, or determination.

Understandably, our internal motivation and willpower might take a back seat to what is dangling in our faces each day.

There's no better example of the contributions of an environment than the classroom. Endless studies (Dorman, Aldridge, & Fraser, 2006; Bucholz & Sheffler, 2009) cite how supportive classrooms where trust, encouragement, and free inquiry reign produce better outcomes and test scores than ones with little or no resources, low teacher morale, and lack of support.

German-American psychologist Kurt Lewin, one of the architects of social psychology, created a theoretical formula that is one of the most famous in the field: $B = f(P,E)$. Lewin's equation simply asserts that behavior (B) is a function (f) of a person (P) within their environment (E). Behavior is a combination of a person's unique attributes with mitigating or encouraging factors in the person's most common physical surroundings. Lewin's dictum flew in the face of commonly accepted theories that claimed a person's *past* was the decisive element of their behavior (Ahem, Freud); he believed that the person's placement in a *current* situation fueled his or her conduct. This is more likely to be true for daily actions and habits, though not necessarily with underlying attachments and emotions.

Environment can, of course, be divided into two entities: physical and social. Physical environmental factors include everything in a given space that one can perceive with the five senses—sound, cleanliness, darkness, or light. As it relates to changing your behavior, this could be something that is physically unavoidable or completely absent—*out of sight, out of mind.* Social factors include everything from the people you surround yourself with, customs, and traditions to communication style, support models, and behavior.

Because an environment is usually perceived as a larger situation someone enters into, one might believe it's impossible to shift the factors within that environment or to change the environment itself. But that's not true. It's entirely achievable to alter and manipulate your physical surroundings and interpersonal relations and to create situations that encourage your success.

Improve Your Environment

Adjusting your environment can make changing your behavior a whole lot easier. A new setting can help you bounce back from fixed ways of thinking you were unaware of and open up completely new avenues that can restore your enthusiasm and stimulate your effort.

This notion may seem disempowering. We'd prefer to think of success as the result of our own hard work—resolve, effort, and determination. Conversely, we fault failure on deficiencies in willpower, ability, talent, or performance. And for sure, all these personal factors count very highly in our accomplishments (or lack thereof).

But when you study how human behavior evolves over a long time period, environment frequently plays more of a part in success than motivation or skill. Environment is the hidden force that guides human behavior. Yes, incentive, aptitude, and labor are important, but these traits often get overmatched by the surroundings in which we dwell.

Habits and behavior argue for the "nurture" end of the "nature-or-nurture" debate—as does environment. External factors are the invisible accomplices for shaping how we react and behave. Over time, the environment conditions our actions and practices on a greater scale than our "natures"—our talents and beliefs—do. And it's possible to tweak those surroundings so we're enabled to use our talents, decision-making skills, and efforts in the most productive way possible.

Design Your Environment for Good Decisions

Brian Wansink of Cornell University conducted a study on dietary habits in 2006 and made an interesting discovery. When people switched from serving plates twelve inches in diameter to plates that were ten inches, they wound up eating 22 percent *less* food. This finding was so effective that nutrition writers have recycled it as a tip for diet success, to the extent that some espouse using tiny plates and tiny portions to curb appetites.

It's a great example of how even a minor adjustment in an environment can contribute to improved decision-making. The change in plate size was a minuscule two inches—not quite the width of a smartphone—but yielded more than one-fifth of a decrease in consumption. Repeated over time, this minor modification can build up good habits to make major impacts.

This practice is far more adaptable and versatile than you might think. The guiding principle is to make your environment more likely to trigger good habits you want to increase and hinder bad habits you want to eliminate—and making sure these triggers fit in the flow of your life.

If you want more incentive to practice a musical instrument, for example, you could make a permanent place for the instrument in the middle of a room with instructions of exactly where to pick up. You could also leave a trail of sheet music that literally requires you to pick it up to walk to your bed. If you want to work out more, you're more likely to visit a gym if it's located on your way home from work, rather than ten miles in the opposite direction.

You can also put your gym bag in front of your front door, buy a pull-up bar for your kitchen doorway, and only wear shoes that can double as exercise shoes. Finally, if you want to procrastinate less, you can leave reminder Post-its next to door handles and your wallet (things you will have to touch), leave your work in a place you can't avoid it, and hide your distracting temptations.

Decreasing bad habits is a function of *out of sight, out of mind*. For example, supermarkets often place higher-priced items at customers' eye levels to increase the chances they'll buy them. But one could *reverse* this process at home by keeping unhealthy foods away from immediate view and storing them in less visible or harder-to-reach levels. Put your chocolate inside five containers like a Russian nesting doll and put them in a closet—see how often you binge then.

To stop smoking, one might consider removing all the ashtrays from inside the home and place them as far away as possible on the perimeter of their property so smoking will necessitate a brisk walk in the freezing winter. To keep from sitting down all day, you can switch to a standing desk that will force you to stand up during most working hours. You could also simply remove chairs and coffee tables from the area in which you do most of your work.

The whole idea is to eliminate having to make decisions, because that's where we usually hit a snag. Depending on willpower and discipline is risky to say the least, so create an environment that will help you automate your decisions and make good habits the default choice. In taking that decision out of your hands, you're rewiring yourself to remove bad habits from your routine—and likely saving a little time in the process.

Author Mihaly Csikszentmihalyi, known for the book *Flow*, calls this general approach for changing environment changing one's *activation energy*—the less activation energy required to make good decisions and form good habits, the better. And by contrast, the higher the activation energy for completing a bad habit, the better. Activation energy can also be seen as the overall amount of effort people are willing to spend. When we make the conscious choice to make harder activities more immediately accessible, they stand better chances of becoming permanent lifestyle changes.

Improving Your Social Support

Setting up your physical environment is a major step and at least somewhat easy to picture—more piano sheet music, less chocolate, more reminders, and fewer distractions. But if you don't have a solid social structure that reinforces your good habits, you're in danger of faltering every time you step out of your environment. That's the negative aspect to manipulating your physical environment—it only works when you're *in* it. Social support, however, is with us day and night.

A recent study by the *New England Journal of Medicine* closely analyzed a social network consisting of 12,067 people. They had been monitored for thirty-two years between 1971 and 2003. Investigators had detailed information on the connections: who were friends, who were spouses, siblings, neighbors, and so forth. They also tracked how much each person in the network weighed at specific times over those three decades.

They found that members of this network tended to gain weight when their friends did, increasing their chances of obesity by 57 percent. This wasn't the case when family members' weights changed; the correlation mainly came from friends and the people they interacted with the most. Whether these friends were located close by or across the country, they maintained the same influence. Very close friends were even likelier to gain weight—if one part of a pair of friends became obese, the other one's chances of becoming obese increased by a whopping 171 percent.

Whether they think they do or not, those around us have a huge influence on our lives. They can support us, discourage us, or remain wholly apathetic to our goals. Any of these can have a lasting effect on whether we are able to reach your definition of success. For instance, say you wanted to learn piano, but three of your close friends announced that piano was for *nerds* and *losers*. How likely is it that you will persist in this goal, knowing the social pressures and stigmas associated with it? We tend to take others' behaviors around us somewhat personally, as a reflection of our friendship.

But like our physical environment, we can change our social environments as well.

When it comes to others' negative attitudes or indifference, it's more about *them*, not us. If they express negativity about what you want, it's probably because they're envious or resentful that they don't have the courage to do what you're doing. If you're nervous and excited about a new job that answers to your interests, they might deflate your excitement because they're stuck in their own rut. If you're enthusiastic about buying your first house, they may bring you down by making disparaging judgments about the neighborhood you're moving to—just because they can't afford to buy a house themselves.

If they're apathetic, that's just a reflection that you're not the main concern in their life. Which is fine—you don't have to be. Your friends may not be as excited as you are about finding a new personal trainer or taking a class to expand your skills, because it's not something terribly important to them. In return, they may not expect you to be over-excited about their new diet or music appreciation class.

None of these attitudes in and of themselves are reasons to end a friendship, but it's possible to surround yourself with a social framework that's more supportive of your needs—and at least cares enough to throw you an encouraging word and ask about your progress occasionally. We can't choose our families, but we can adjust our friendship circles to be conducive to our goals.

In particular, we can keep an eye out for social members who can fill specific roles in our support environment.

Accountability partner. This is a person who shares your successes, acts as a motivator, and keep you on course. This is someone you report (daily, weekly, monthly) to so you can make sure you're doing what you should be doing, and they do the same. You share each other's challenges, concerns, and victories, and you regenerate each other through work challenges, family situations, health issues, daily practical matters, ambitions, and goals.

They're also a sounding board of ideas and experience, as you are with them. The chances for mutual growth with an accountability partner are excellent.

Mentors, role models, and teachers. There are likely at least one or two people we hold up as examples of who we'd like to be. While this kind of admiration shouldn't translate into meaningless hero worship, there's good reason to spend as much time as you can with these people to see their habits in action. Observe their best practices and mindsets, and practice emulating them to see how it affects your behavior. Even seek to connect with them and ask for direct guidance.

Of course, there's a chance that they may not be everything you thought they were—which is fine. They don't have to be superheroes, and seeing them as normal people might make your journey more navigable and approachable. Just keep in mind that you can learn from them in a few specific ways, so pay attention.

New people. An interesting theory is that you're the average of the five people you spend the most time with. They could be all the same kind of people or wildly different from each other, but they have significant influence on your thoughts and deeds. The implication is that we are truly products of our social environments, and we pick up an immeasurable number of thoughts just being in the presence of people.

Is this fact positive or negative? That's what you have to find out. You never want to be the most superlative positive member—the "smartest," the "prettiest," the "richest"—of any given group—because that means the averages of the other people are dragging you down. This isn't meant to sound judgmental or catty; it's just that if you truly want to prioritize achieving your goals and expanding in substantial ways, you may need to find another group to spend time with. Surround yourself with better piano players, smarter businesspeople, or more disciplined entrepreneurs.

This is an inherently uncomfortable process because it likely involves you seeking out intimidating people and the realization that you are now a small fish in a large pond. But it's part of the process of moving onward and upward. Don't abandon your friends, your social network, or your groups; just understand the power of the people around you.

Keep yourself low-maintenance. There's as much value—more, potentially—in receiving passive support from your network, so let them know they don't have to exert too much effort beyond consistent emotional support. There's really nothing much to that kind of support at all; it's relatively easy to dispense and doesn't wear others out. Just let them know they're important to you and that you value them whether they're involved in your everyday existence or if they're further away. The residual support may be enough to get you through without their lifting a finger.

The task of altering our environments shouldn't be as onerous as it looks on paper. Most of the effort consists of small but meaningful adjustments that change the flow around you, just enough to start new patterns and change your behavior for the better.

Takeaways:

- The environments we find ourselves in have a startling ability to influence whether or not we reach our goals. Environments can be encouraging or discouraging, or they make matters flat-out possible or impossible.

- Environment can be split into the physical environment and social environment. Both matter, though the influence of the physical can be said to be restrained to when you are *in* it.

- To manipulate your physical environment for greater success, you want to make it easier and require less *activation energy* to complete good habits while making it more difficult for bad habits to persist. This is for the purpose of making good decisions your easiest default action.

- Manipulating your social environment is more difficult but possibly more effective because it stays with you day and night. You are the average of the five people you spend the most time with, so you can look into finding an accountability partner, mentors, role models, and overall new people to connect with.

Chapter 6. Design Flaws in Habit Formation

At the start of this book, we began with an unavoidable truth: that people find it exceptionally hard to change. Do you recall the study that discovered that people try an average of ten times to break a bad habit or learn a new one?

We've delved into what propels behavior change: why people act in the ways that they do. We've examined how we can control our brain chemistry and psychology and exploit them for our improvement. Even with all this new and powerful knowledge, pitfalls could arise. If you've come up with a faulty or ineffective plan focused on the wrong habits or made a strategic error, you might not succeed in making the changes you're seeking.

That's why this chapter takes a look at some common design flaws that can derail your efforts in changing behavior—or keep you on the same track on which change never occurs. But as with the rest of this book, we can take a flaw or weakness and, with conscious awareness, commitment and understanding, transform it into something that works for us rather than against us.

B.J. Fogg's Mistakes for Change

Fogg identified some common mistakes in thinking, framing, and approaching behavioral change—and how to adapt one's way of thinking to correct course and push change forward.

Relying on willpower for long-term change. Willpower, for all its merits, is a finite and inconstant resource. You can regenerate it, of course, but you can't rely on raw will to lead you through a protracted period of behavioral change.

Trying to keep an exercise program, a diet, or system of work discipline going through sheer will alone could deplete the mental faculties that control will and lead to what scientists call "ego depletion."

Fogg's solution is to pretend that willpower isn't even an available option. Instead, narrow your focus on the smaller behavior changes that can lead to eventual development of larger-scale transformations—build your new behavior brick by brick, from the ground up. This is why its so important to manipulate your environment to support positive behaviors.

Attempting big leaps instead of baby steps. We tend to focus on change as an overwhelming, major event—not a series of smaller steps that lead practically to a positive solution. We celebrate when a baseball team wins the World Series, not when they win the first game of spring training.

That view undermines the truth that it takes a lot of smaller work for change to be successful, and it can distort our strategy.

We feel underwhelmed when we've lost only one pound over the course of a week or when we don't have complete knowledge of a school subject after reading the material only once. This could lead us to overshoot our ambitions too early and attempt to crank major efforts out in less time than anyone possibly can.

Again, Fogg urges us to focus on the smaller picture and celebrate the miniature progress we make step by step. Realizing the larger goal is fine, but building new behaviors relies on the accumulation of smaller but still significant victories. Everything starts with something small, and sometimes it's hard to see how it can contribute to the end goal—but it can and does.

Trying to stop old behaviors instead of creating new ones. Successfully stopping a bad habit by going "cold turkey" is more the exception than the rule. We make vows to stop smoking or drinking by shutting consumption down completely. But this frequently fails because we haven't come up with an answer for the cravings we feel;

we've just told ourselves we're going to deal with the discomfort without knowing how. Your brain is still expecting to be satisfied with the behavior you're cutting off, and your brain is not happy about this.

The solution is to replace the old behavior or routine with a new one—but one that delivers some kind of compensatory reward that the brain can understand. If you're trying to give up sugary sweets but your brain craves the reward, try eating a piece of healthy fruit. If you're craving a cigarette, try finding a motor activity—playing piano, housecleaning, or building furniture—that gives you a sense of accomplishment. Simply telling someone to stop indulging is tough; replacing that feeling is both more productive and sustainable.

Believing that information leads to action. I really hope you've enjoyed this book and that it gave you a lot of valuable information. But you're not done, even though this book nearly is.

Knowing the facts about a certain situation does not equal working on it. You can tell someone why it's important to stop smoking, exercise, or increase their attention span, but that's not sufficient stimuli in and of itself. Rationalization is almost always useless; there needs to be a motivating action as well.

Instead of gathering more intel on what you need to do, begin applying the information in real situations. Focus on identifying your triggers, adjusting your patterns, putting in the effort, and recording your results on a regular basis. As Mike Tyson once said, *"Everyone has a plan until they get punched in the face."* Your plans, based on all the information you've gathered, might be useless once you start and realize they won't work for you. Leap before you look occasionally.

Seeking to change a behavior forever, not for a short time. This is similar to the second of Fogg's flaws: trying to make huge changes instead of smaller ones. Instead of the *size* of the change, this failing concerns the *time* element. Making overly ambitious proclamations that we'll banish the bad and embrace the good until the end of time distorts the reality of change—again, that it's the culmination of several small changes executed faithfully over an extended period of time. This is why twelve-step programs focus on the "now" and tracking progress "one day at a time."

The solution to this problem is at least a little obvious: limit the range of time you're focusing on and accept the accomplishment of changing on a smaller scale and a day-by-day frame of mind. Don't try to eat the whole pie at once because you'll defeat yourself mentally. Just take it one slice at a time, focus on the present, and see what you can do to keep moving forward. With behavior and habits, just focus on what you can do at the present moment.

James Clear's Mistakes That Cause New Habits to Fail

James Clear "studies successful people across a wide range of disciplines... to uncover the habits and routines that make these people the best at what they do." He shares his findings in a popular newsletter.

After a few years of careful inspection, Clear uncovered some typical mistakes that keep new habits from taking root in people trying to change their behavior. Clear and Fogg offer some similar perspectives on these mistakes, but Clear identifies two more common errors committed by those seeking to alter their behaviors and habits.

Seeking a result, not a ritual. We tend to value the *payoff* in contemporary society. We're looking to lose a hundred pounds, increase our productivity by 110 percent, finish first in the marathon, and, if we have time, stave off death forever. We may value effort, but if it doesn't produce the results we want exactly as we want them, we consider that effort to have failed.

The problem with this, Clear says, is that "New goals don't deliver new results. New lifestyles do." For this reason, he suggests envisioning behavior change as something that happens every day—as a ritual.

Over time and repetition, these rituals add up and produce solid lifestyle changes. It may be frustrating that we don't see immediate effects from a day or two of changing behavior. But we can gauge progress more incrementally—after a year, a month, or even a week.

The trick is putting your thoughts, emotions, and efforts into keeping the ritual. Focus on the fifteen-minute jog, the twenty minutes of meditation, the thirty minutes of studying, or the hour of music practice that you repeat every day. You can refine or add to those rituals as you keep them up—but keep your mind oriented on the routine in and of itself.

Assuming small changes don't add up. In a similar vein, our focus on big payoffs often conjures up an idea of the minimum that we want to accomplish. In addition to the hundred pounds we want to lose, mentioned above, we want to successfully complete three semesters of five classes each, make $50,000 in commissions, and sew a hundred uniforms for our children's high school marching band. With all these grand schemes, we tend to downgrade the asset of patience.

Clear says this leads us to believe that "achievements need to be big to make a difference." But again, in reality the habits we have today are the accrual of the good and bad options we've selected over years and years.

Similar to developing rituals, Clear suggests centering on small changes and developing them over a series of time to enable wholesale habit changes down the road. "Build the behavior first," Clear says. "Worry about the results later."

Takeaways:

- The psychological design flaws we encounter in changing our behaviors take several predictable forms. B.J. Fogg articulated a few: relying on willpower and discipline, shooting for big steps rather than small, trying to stop old behaviors rather than start new ones, believing that information without action leads to change, and attempting to change a behavior forever rather than just for today.

- James Clear also articulated two design flaws in changing our behavior: seeking a result above all else, and assuming small changes don't add up.

Summary Guide

CHAPTER 1. A PEEK INTO THE SCIENCE OF HABITS

- Habits are repeated, learned behaviors, but they have neurochemical and physiological correlates in the brain.
- Your brain possesses the characteristic of plasticity—i.e., neural pathways can be rewired and old habits can be replaced with new ones. This is what makes it possible for us to learn, adapt and change.
- There are three steps to habit formation: the **trigger** which signals the brain to go into "autopilot" mode, the **routine** behavior itself, and the **reward** that follows and reinforces the behavior.
- The above process is mediated by dopamine, which forms the neurochemical basis for our reward

system. When dopamine is released, we form memories of what was pleasurable and felt good, so we're more likely to repeat those behaviors.

- Other hormones like serotonin, GABA and norepinephrine modulate the balance between goal-directed or habit-directed brain modes.

- If we want to change our bad habits, we need to work with our innate brain mechanisms.

- The pleasure principle is a simple but powerful fundamental motivator of all human (and animal!) behavior. It states that humans are motivated to act in ways that reduce pain and suffering and maximize pleasure.

- The pleasure principle is an evolutionary fact that's all about survival, but it also means that we work harder to avoid pain than we do to seek out pleasure. This may explain why it's hard to proactively make positive changes in life, but relatively easy to avoid massively negative habits.

- Emotion trumps all: what we *perceive* as pleasurable is what matters, and this inevitably means we focus on the present, and ignore long-term outcomes and consequences—another reason that permanent behavioral change is difficult.

- To get rid of unwanted bad behaviors and develop healthy new ones, we need to understand what habits are, learn how they form, and work with our inbuilt tendencies to make lasting changes.

CHAPTER 2. HABIT FORMATION PSYCHOLOGY

- Forming new habits has a physiological, psychological and a behavioral component. By understanding the psychology of the way habits are made and broken, we can work to create better ones.

- A behavior needs to be uniform, repeated regularly, and must automatically follow a trigger in the environment. It takes no conscious effort. Establishing behaviors may be difficult to begin with, but becomes easier with time; likewise they may not be enjoyable at first, but can become more so with time.

- By understanding the three-step loop of habit formation, we can create the environment needed to support new habits, while discouraging old ones.

- There are different types of habits, and they can each have both advantages and disadvantages, whether they're "good" or "bad."

- Even though we logically and intellectually know what we should do, why don't do we those things? Because despite what we like to think, we aren't really operating on conscious free will most of the time. There are three categories of obstacles to doing what we truly want at any point: *conscious, subconscious,* and *external* factors.

- Conscious factors are ones we know and readily tell ourselves. They are what we repeat when we fail or decide not to do something. They include low self-esteem, negative self-image, over-tolerance of pain or discomfort, aversion to confrontation, and fear of failure and rejection.

- Subconscious factors are similar to the conscious factors, yet they are so deeply ingrained in our identities we don't even realize we hold these beliefs—they are just our automatic thought patterns. They include limiting beliefs and narratives, having a fixed mindset, and being victim to traumatic experiences.

- External factors are outside of ourselves. They are the environmental or social pressures that keep us from taking action. Some of these are legitimate; some are simply excuses. These include lack of knowledge, too many obligations, being too comfortable, harmful environments, social inertia, or rejection.

CHAPTER 3. THE FRAMEWORK FOR LASTING CHANGE

- Your brain cannot tell the difference between a healthy or unhealthy habit—habits are habits, and they're formed in exactly the same way.

- We can only change habits when we make the unconscious conscious, and take deliberate control over the automatic processes that lead to habit formation.

- Habits are small but cumulative in their effect—bad habits undermine our health, relationships, and performance while good habits develop good character, success and well-being, fostering a "virtuous cycle" that leads to further good habits.

- To build a good habit, we need to examine the three-step loop in our own behavior and work to make changes at each level.

- Identify a habit that you wish to develop and look closely for possible preceding triggers and the following reward that reinforces it via the dopamine-based reward system.

- Now, build the trigger into your own life, ensuring you're rewarding yourself to cement the habit every time you follow through with the behavior. Keep repeating the same behavior in the same environmental context, and track your progress.

- A new behavior takes time to take root, so you need patience and dedication in the meantime.

- There are dozens of scientifically proven techniques to encourage habit formation, but they are all variations of the three-step loop. When trying to develop a new habit, keep consistent and repeat as often as possible, plan ahead consciously, introduce cues and prompts, and break down bigger goals into smaller, more manageable milestones.

- When trying to break a bad habit, remember to address the physical, emotional, psychological, behavioral and environmental factors, too.

- When deciding on an appropriate technique for habit formation, first identify your overall goal, then outline the three steps of trigger, habit and reward, so you can make changes at each step.

CHAPTER 4. MORE OF THE GOOD, LESS OF THE BAD

- Habits are mental heuristics designed to save mental energy, time and effort—you don't need sheer force or willpower to develop good habits, only an understanding of how they naturally develop, plus enough commitment and discipline to stick to the plan you choose for yourself.
- It's OK to make mistakes, to be lazy or feel unmotivated, but with good habits what matters is staying consistent, no matter what.
- Small incremental changes that add up are the key to reaching big goals; our focus should be on process and not outcome.
- Making yourself accountable to others by sharing your commitment makes it more likely that you will

maintain your habit and achieve your goal.

- A keystone habit is a meta-habit that inspires many smaller, related habits. By focusing on the development of the keystone habit that matters most to you, you don't need to work to build dozens of smaller habits.
- Keystone habits can be physical, intellectual, emotional or spiritual, and they ultimately encourage the cultivation of a stronger, happier and more resilient character.
- Breaking bad habits is difficult but not impossible. Since many of us are oblivious to the existence of our bad habits, we need honesty and self-awareness to become conscious of why we're really behaving as we are.
- To identify a bad habit, look for defense mechanisms like over-rationalizing, cognitive dissonance, emotional irregularity, automatic behavior you can't seem to control, and negative effects to your health, relationships or work life.

- You can use positive reinforcement, negative reinforcement or punishment to move yourself away from a bad habit, i.e. increasing the pain or decreasing the pleasure associated with the habit, or else increasing the pleasure associated with an alternative habit. Manipulating triggers and rewards allows you to decrease the likelihood of the behavior recurring.

- It's easier to replace a habit than to eliminate it. Keep the trigger and reward the same but replace the habit itself with a more positive one.

CHAPTER 5. HOW TO SHORT CIRCUIT YOURSELF

- The environments we find ourselves in have a startling ability to influence whether or not we reach our goals. Environments can be encouraging or discouraging, or they make matters flat-out possible or impossible.

- Environment can be split into the physical environment and social environment. Both matter, though the influence of the physical can be said to be restrained to when you are *in* it.
- To manipulate your physical environment for greater success, you want to make it easier and require less *activation energy* to complete good habits while making it more difficult for bad habits to persist. This is for the purpose of making good decisions your easiest default action.
- Manipulating your social environment is more difficult but possibly more effective because it stays with you day and night. You are the average of the five people you spend the most time with, so you can look into finding an accountability partner, mentors, role models, and overall new people to connect with.

CHAPTER 6. DESIGN FLAWS IN HABIT FORMATION

- The psychological design flaws we encounter in changing our behaviors take several predictable forms. B.J. Fogg articulated a few: relying on willpower and discipline, shooting for big steps rather than small, trying to stop old behaviors rather than start new ones, believing that information without action leads to change, and attempting to change a behavior forever rather than just for today.

- James Clear also articulated two design flaws in changing our behavior: seeking a result above all else, and assuming small changes don't add up.

Made in the USA
Middletown, DE
27 June 2023